END OF THE LINE

THE PUBLISHER AND AUTHOR ARE GRATEFUL TO THE
WILSON INSTITUTE FOR CANADIAN HISTORY
AT MCMASTER UNIVERSITY FOR AWARDING DUNDURN
THE FIRST WILSON PRIZE FOR PUBLISHING CANADIAN HISTORY.
THIS SUPPORT ENABLED US TO PUBLISH THIS SIGNIFICANT BOOK.

END OF THE LINE
The 1857 Train Wreck at the Desjardins Canal Bridge

Don McIver

DUNDURN
TORONTO

Copyright © Don McIver, 2013

All rights reserved. No part of this publication may be reproduced, stored in a retrieval system, or transmitted in any form or by any means, electronic, mechanical, photocopying, recording, or otherwise (except for brief passages for purposes of review) without the prior permission of Dundurn Press. Permission to photocopy should be requested from Access Copyright.

Editor: Cheryl Hawley
Design: Jesse Hooper
Printer: Webcom

Library and Archives Canada Cataloguing in Publication

McIver, Don
    End of the line : the 1857 train wreck at the Desjardins Canal bridge / by Don McIver.

Includes bibliographical references and index.
Issued also in electronic formats.
ISBN 978-1-4597-0222-6

    1. Railroad accidents--Ontario--Hamilton. 2. Great Western Railway Company (Canada)--History. I. Title.

HE1783.C3M33 2013   363.12'20971352   C2012-900147-3

1 2 3 4 5   17 16 15 14 13

We acknowledge the support of the **Canada Council for the Arts** and the **Ontario Arts Council** for our publishing program. We also acknowledge the financial support of the **Government of Canada** through the **Canada Book Fund** and **Livres Canada Books**, and the **Government of Ontario** through the **Ontario Book Publishing Tax Credit** and the **Ontario Media Development Corporation**.

Care has been taken to trace the ownership of copyright material used in this book. The author and the publisher welcome any information enabling them to rectify any references or credits in subsequent editions.
  J. Kirk Howard, President

VISIT US AT
Dundurn.com | Definingcanada.ca | @dundurnpress | Facebook.com/dundurnpress

Dundurn	Gazelle Book Services Limited	Dundurn
3 Church Street, Suite 500	White Cross Mills	2250 Military Road
Toronto, Ontario, Canada	High Town, Lancaster, England	Tonawanda, NY
M5E 1M2	L41 4XS	U.S.A. 14150

CONTENTS

Acknowledgements	7
Preface	9
Chapter One: Slow Train to Eternity	13
Chapter Two: The Next Few Moments	25
Chapter Three: The Day Dawned Clear	41
Chapter Four: One Bold Operator	53
Chapter Five: A Cast of Players	71
Chapter Six: Great Western Railway: Financial Fits and Starts	95
Chapter Seven: Great Western Railway: Shovel Ready at Last	121
Chapter Eight: Bridges and Brydges	149
Chapter Nine: The Inquest	169
Epilogue	195
A Note on Sources	201
Index	207

To my wife, Anya, and my son, Daniel

ACKNOWLEDGEMENTS

Every author benefits from the contributions of others. Sometimes it may be no more than an interested response to an enthusiastic recounting of a single element of the story or a comment that helps the writer avoid the risk of becoming too immersed in detail. Others have provided continuous encouragement. To all those who have supported this initiative I am very grateful.

Today, newsworthy events are documented with a flood of instantaneous images. The episodes described in *End of the Line* occurred when photography was in its infancy. Those illustrations that have survived add immeasurably to the poignant authenticity of events as they unfolded a century and a half ago and I am greatly appreciative of those who helped make their inclusion possible.

Mac Swackhammer of the Hamilton Museum of Steam and Technology supplied the cover illustration that so perfectly captures the mood the morning after the disaster. Margaret Houghton, enthusiastic author and archivist with the Hamilton Public Library, generously provided material from the library's collection. Cathy Roy and Andrew Porteus with the Niagara Falls Public Library helped illustrate aspects of Samuel Zimmerman's remarkable career in that city.

Hamilton's major historic site, Dundurn Castle, stands literally within eyesight of the fateful bridge over the Desjardins Canal and the man who built the elaborate mansion was intimately involved in the affairs of the railway. Dundurn's curators Kenneth Heaman and Tom Minnes, along with Richard Barlas with Hamilton's Culture Division, helped identify and provide some fascinating glimpses of the wonderful world that the castle represented.

Molly Hawkins, the great-granddaughter of Adam Ferrie's young widow, kindly provided some of the family history and her cousin Tom Stewart was able to provide the illustration of Mary Dallas later in life.

Rick Berketa of Niagara Falls solved my problem of obtaining a photograph of the Zimmerman gravesite by simply driving to the graveyard with his camera.

I would like to extend gratitude to Barry and Jane Penhale for their invaluable advice and to Cheryl Hawley for the comprehensive, but extremely sensitive, job of text editing.

To these, and the many others who have helped with this project, I express my thanks. I would especially like to note the support provided by my family.

PREFACE

The mid-nineteenth century arrival of the railways was transformative and traumatic. The way that people lived and worked, and how they interacted with the world outside their community, had probably never been more swiftly and permanently altered. The early railways brought efficiency and abruptly kickstarted industrial expansion. However, they also placed previously unheard of demands on the rudimentary engineering of the day. Each year the trains got faster and heavier, quickly exposing the crudeness of materials and the absence of scientific method in the design and maintenance of structures and equipment. When the early railways failed, they did so spectacularly.

Mass death was not uncommon in the mid-nineteenth century. Disease was badly misunderstood and, for the most part, remedies were rudimentary or simply unavailable. Cholera, exported from famine-swept Ireland and nurtured by weeks of inhuman seaboard conditions, swept through the new world, killing thousands. Survivors of everyday accidents endured hours or days of excruciating travel to reach medical care that consisted of little more than staunching, amputation, bed rest, and prayer. Shipwrecks were commonplace. Death tolls in the hundreds were surprisingly frequent. The newspapers contained many more stories of calamitous loss of life at sea than we read of disastrous air crashes today.

But death by train was something different. It was sudden — one minute you were riding comfortably, the next you were catapulted into the hereafter or trapped in excruciating pain. It was over almost before it had begun. Before there was time to understand what was happening, the train was wrecked and the lottery decided who walked away, who was injured, and who was past help. Unlike shipwrecks that occurred off remote coasts, railway accidents frequently happened in places where spectators and rescuers could congregate before the steam had cooled and the hot metal had stopped contracting. The victims were often local — friends and neighbours of the rescuers.

Railway death and injury was frighteningly modern. The railway changed the community, brought in new values and undermined the old. Trains brought in outside commercial and cultural influences, which challenged local interests. Probably the biggest challenge to conventional values of the time was railway companies running trains on Sundays.

Early railway disasters often took on almost mythical significance, ballads were written and legends born. The most likely to be etched into folk consciousness involved bridges. It is not hard to understand why. Trains meandering at an often sedate pace across the level countryside promised a sporting chance of survival when they derailed. Bridge wrecks offered less generous odds.

The story of the wreck of a Great Western Railway of Canada train that collapsed the wooden swing bridge over the Desjardins Canal in Hamilton, Ontario, and plunged to the canal's frozen surface, killing sixty, is an archetype of the railway bridge disaster genre. The site of the accident — which was one of the most deadly experienced anywhere in North America at that time — is remarkably accessible today. Each year millions of travellers cross the short stretch of canal by superhighway, city street, and commuter train within view of the location.

Preface

The whole episode is rife with irony. Any major catastrophe spawns a host of might-have-beens — people who just missed being there, or those who just managed to be there and paid the consequence. But for high irony it is difficult to match the quirk of fate that had Samuel Zimmerman, the general contractor for that section of the Great Western, die in the accident. Compound that with the widely held view that Zimmerman delivered slipshod results at inflated prices and that many believed that he had skimped on the construction of the bridge itself. It wasn't long before contemporaries like the cantankerous William Lyon Mackenzie were unctuously revelling in the notion that Zimmerman was literally hoist with his own petard! The second irony was that the bridge was, in fact, designed by a man of unquestioned technical merit who came to be viewed as the father of scientific bridge construction in North America — and he stood steadfastly behind the bridge's integrity.

This chronicle details the precursors and immediate causes, as well as the subsequent impact on the community. Then goes further, to examine the lives and deaths of many of the passengers who represent a fascinating cross-section of a population that couldn't have existed only a few years earlier and contrasts markedly with the stereotypical view of how Canadians lived in the 1850s.

CHAPTER ONE

SLOW TRAIN TO ETERNITY

Late in the afternoon of March 12, 1857, the Great Western Railway train for Hamilton stood at the line's temporary Toronto terminus at the foot of Bathurst Street. Shortly after 4:00 p.m. Samuel Zimmerman hauled himself aboard. Despite the early signs of a paunch — the consequence of an appetite for the very best in refreshment — Sam, just short of his forty-second birthday and recently married to a woman many years his junior, was assuredly in the prime of his life. No further triumphs would be possible because he, along with the majority of his fellow travellers, had less than two hours left to live.

Zimmerman was in a convivial mood; he nearly always was. He was a most hospitable man by nature — his wide-flung business interests and his generosity were legendary, and intertwined. He had travelled the short distance from a local hotel to the station by horse-drawn cab in the company of representatives of the Canada Southern Railway. They had passed the previous hours hammering out final arrangements for the construction of the Canada Southern, a line intended to provide serious competition for the Great Western. Zimmerman had the new charter in his pocket. His role as one of the chief contractors of the Great Western had contributed massively to his considerable affluence, and he had no ill will toward the Great Western, but Zimmerman was not one to dwell on the past when there was new money and more friends to be won.

Among those who travelled to the station with Zimmerman was Captain Henry Twohy. Although he had no reason to board the train he seemed to have been caught up in the general enthusiasm of the moment and, doubtless influenced by the flow of spirits that lubricated most business dealings of the time, he accepted the boisterous invitations of his friends to continue the celebration in Hamilton. Perhaps the sharp chill of the cab ride helped sober him a little or perhaps, as he later claimed, he really did remember previous commitments. In either case, he made his excuses, left the train, and almost certainly saved his own life.

As departure time approached, the two passenger cars began to fill. The stuffy heat of the wood-burning stoves offered a welcome relief from the still-freezing mid-March temperatures on the unprotected

By the time of this 1867 photograph the Great Western Railway's Toronto station had been established at the foot of Yonge Street. Ten years earlier trains were departing from a temporary platform at Queen's Quay, before the line was extended from the outskirts.
PUBLIC DOMAIN.

platform. Among the other passengers was Thomas Street, a well-known financier and former member of Parliament. While Zimmerman would have contended he was the wealthiest man in Canada, some suspected the claim owed more to his flair for self-promotion. If Zimmerman wasn't the richest Canadian, then Thomas C. Street might have been. Both Zimmermann and Street lived in Clifton (today Niagara Falls, Ontario), and both had been highly influential in the commercial development of that city. But there the similarity ended. Street was every inch the pragmatic and low-key patrician. Zimmerman, on the other hand, flaunted his deal-making triumphs and revelled in his influence. To use a modern-day analogy, contrast the quietly assured financier Warren Buffet with the personality of real-estate tycoon Donald Trump. Sam was "The Donald" of his time. Although the men obviously knew each other, Street chose to sit in the leading passenger car — Zimmerman in the rear car.

Among the other passengers was a well-known ship's captain, turned wealthy shipping magnate, James Sutherland. Also boarding in Toronto were the recently married son of Hamilton's first mayor, a number of off-duty railway officials, and a cross-section of the newly mobile public.

As the time for departure neared, engineer Alexander Burnfield dropped from the warmth of his cab and made the mandatory trip around the locomotive armed with a hammer, which he dutifully tapped against each of the wheels. The standard test of the cast-iron wheels relied on a clear bell tone to indicate soundness. If the metal was cracked — even if the blemish was not visible — the hammer would make a duller noise. The engineer was quickly satisfied that the engine passed the routine examination, hardly surprising since the imposing engine Oxford had only recently been returned to service after a complete overhaul.

Burnfield clambered back aboard and peered back through the escaping steam to await Conductor Barrett's final bellowed "ALL ABOARD!" and permission to get underway. That received, he gave a last blast on his whistle and eased open the throttle.

END OF THE LINE

The 4:10 to Hamilton was scarcely an express hell-bent for eternity. Scheduled at a respectable, albeit leisurely pace that would see it reach Hamilton roughly two hours later, it ambled over the flat plains north of Lake Ontario stopping at all local stations. Still, although advertised as an "accommodation" train, it was by no means intended to attract the rustic provincial traveller. The train consisted of a leading baggage car and two first-class cars. The Great Western was never mean in its accommodation — it was, after all, the first railway in the world to introduce a sleeping car.

Great Western Railway locomotive Spitfire, a contemporary to the ill-fated Oxford, was typical of the 4-4-0 locomotives built in North America during the early years of railroading.

U.S. LIBRARY OF CONGRESS, LC-USZ62-93788.

Although most passengers intended to make the complete Toronto to Hamilton trip, the train stopped at Mimico, Port Credit, Oakville, Bronte, Wellington Square, and Waterdown to drop off or pick up passengers. At Wellington Square Alfred Booker climbed on board. Booker was a fire-and-brimstone evangelical Baptist, of the old school — a man who would not flinch from casting the mote from the eye of an offending brother. Every inch the archetypical Victorian cleric, the feisty Booker had presided over a late afternoon outreach ministry in neighboring Wellington (now a part of Burlington, Ontario) and was on his way home for a deserved rest. On the platform he would have passed a gentleman who stepped down to take a "breath of air," though more likely he either felt the need to clear his head of the effects of the travellers' comfort or to augment his supply. In either case, he was sufficiently befuddled that when the train left it did so without him. He might be excused if the thought of what might have become of him had he stayed abroad led him to drink. At that point, the majority of those on board had only about fifteen minutes to live.

A few minutes later the complement was approaching the boundary between modern-day Burlington and Hamilton, where the track layout became a little complex. The main line of the Great Western stretched from Niagara Falls to Windsor — the line between Toronto and Hamilton was an offshoot of that central route, added a few years later. The peculiar geography of the western end of Lake Ontario makes Hamilton a natural intermediate station along a straight line linking Niagara and the west. Building the line from Niagara to Hamilton was relatively easy. The direct approach to Hamilton, however, required some pretty heavy engineering.

The city sits at the mouth of the Dundas Valley — a giant cleft in the Niagara Escarpment, several miles across. This formation is riddled with small creeks gushing from the side of the almost vertical walls of the escarpment, like miniature Niagara Falls. Toward the western end of the valley's mouth the creeks accumulate into the shallow marshland known as Cootes Paradise. At its eastern end, the valley exits into one of the very best natural harbours in the Great Lakes. Separating that harbour from both lake and marsh are two narrow ribbons of land. Closest to Lake Ontario is the "Beach Strip," an exaggerated three-mile long sandbar that provides effective shelter from the storms of Lake Ontario. Between harbour and marsh, at the western end, is a more substantial formation known as the Burlington Heights. The Heights constitute a 300-foot-high natural embankment blocking most of the mouth of the Dundas Valley. At the northern end, however, it collapses into a swampy morass through which the waters of Cootes Paradise could seep into the bay.

To satisfy the financial interests of the line's promoters, the engineers of the Great Western chose to approach the city along the northern boundary of Cootes Paradise. That entailed carving a rock ledge into the escarpment and gradually dropping the line so that it was only fifty to a hundred feet above the level of the lake at the point where the Heights fell off. Having skirted the Heights, the line could then be built just above water level, passing beneath Sir Allan MacNab's elegant "castle" to the wharves and terminus at the western end of Hamilton Harbour.

Although the plan entailed some pretty heavy construction, the only major difficulty was dealing with the swampy ground where the Heights petered out. Through this spot the Desjardins Canal Company had expanded the Grindstone Creek to enable their boats to reach the harbour from Cootes Paradise. After abandoning an expensive attempt to bridge the swamp, the railway company made an offer. In exchange for the right to a solid embankment closing-off the canal company's route, the railway would provide a new route by boldly cutting through the middle of the Heights. Part of this agreement required the Great Western to build two new bridges over the new cut — a "high level" suspension bridge for carriages and wagons and a low-level swing bridge to carry the railway into Hamilton.

Satisfactory as this solution was for all concerned, it left the railway with one small problem. In order to gain access to the swing bridge, trains from the west had to navigate a sharp curve, constituting an almost ninety-degree turn. Even today trains take this curve dead slow, accompanied by the screeching of wheel on rail. Without effective competition, the resulting delay must have barely been an irritant to the Great Western. However, the construction of the Toronto and Hamilton Railway introduced a further complication. That line approached the city almost in line with the swing bridge, which it shared with the Great Western main line. At a point only a few hundred feet north of the Desjardins Canal Bridge, the railway installed a switch merging the London and Toronto routes into the solitary pair of metals laid across the bridge. While there were a multitude of contributory factors to the disaster, that switch, placed where it was, sealed the fate of the train's passengers and crew.

The train that approached that switch in the late afternoon of March 12, 1857, was about to demonstrate how a long chain of decisions — some made years earlier, some days before, and some mere moments earlier — can combine to produce disaster. The determination to build the railway and to locate the crossing of the canal

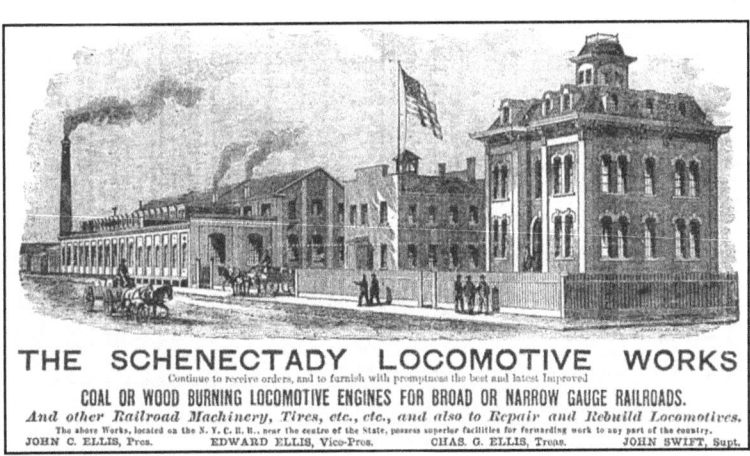

Schenectady Locomotive Works, where the fatal engine Oxford was built. The building at the left in the 1870s advertisement would have been where assembly took place in 1853. The Schenectady plant was later absorbed into one of the most famous locomotive builders: The American Locomotive Company (ALCO).

PUBLIC DOMAIN.

at that precise point, the choice of equipment manufacturer, bridge designer, railway contractor, etc., the decision to move the engine slowly forward without coming to a complete stop at the switch. For the passengers, the choice to travel or not, for some of the crew, the decision to step on or off, determined individual destinies.

The magnificent locomotive at the head of the train had been manufactured by the Schenectady Locomotive Works expressly for the GWR. The twenty-three-ton engine was resplendent in the company's green livery and had only a few days earlier been returned to service after an extensive six-week refit. The wood-burner sported the massive spark-arresting stack and imposing headlight so characteristic of North American engines of the time. With two huge coupled driving wheels on either side — each the height of a tall man — and a leading four-wheel "pony truck" designed to help hold the engine on the line's indifferent track, the Oxford would have been an impressive sight. She would also have sported a sturdy cowcatcher — an absolute essential on the Great Western.

No records survive of Oxford's comprehensive refit at the Great Western's Hamilton shops but it is known that the axle was examined and showed no sign of imperfections. It was not replaced. In light of ensuing events it is a safe bet that it harboured a hidden defect that escaped attention. In an era of soft iron, such components wore easily and required frequent changes. But, it was more than just wear that caused problems with heavy metal pieces. The casting process was crude. Impurities were captured in the web of cooling metal and uneven temperatures led to many castings being rendered unusable by obvious cracks and fissures. Others, while visibly satisfactory, harboured hidden blemishes that would only reveal themselves under the stress of working conditions. Engineer Burnfield's practiced hammer could reveal the subtle difference in ring between a sound wheel and one in which such a fault was beginning to emerge. However, the immense weight of the axle casting made detection far more difficult.

Such a fault clearly existed in Oxford's front axle. Somewhere along the route the fissure lengthened and eventually the axle cracked into two pieces. Probably the only evidence would have been a grinding sound inaudible above the clanking, roaring, vibrating racket of a steam locomotive in motion. Despite the break, the locomotive held the track. When the axle was examined after the accident it was determined that the fracture was fresh and that the two broken ends, held together by the tracks on either side, had grated against each other for some time — rounding the ends and inescapably shortening them.

Although not constrained by the sharp curve the mainline trains had to negotiate, the Toronto to Hamilton train slowed almost to a standstill as it approached the Desjardins Canal Bridge. In the wake of serious accidents in which trains had rushed into open drawbridges, government regulations actually required all trains to come to a complete halt for three minutes before advancing over a draw or swing bridge. Astoundingly, only two years earlier the GWR had managed to secure legislative sanction to ignore that provision. Had the train obeyed the regulation it is almost certain the accident would have been averted. That is not to deny that the train was advancing at no more than a walking pace when it passed the critical switch. In fact, it was the custom of the switchman, who was ending his shift, to hitch a ride by clambering aboard the rear car as it passed. Had it been doing much more than six-miles-per-hour he would not have been able to. As it was, no sooner had he pulled himself onto the bottom step than he dropped off again. Something was not right!

Most likely the sudden shift in gauge caused by the blade of the switch caused the broken axle to twist out of line close to the left-hand front wheel. The right wheel, still attached to its section of axle, mounted the rail and dropped on the outside. Just a few feet from the bridge, engineer Alexander Burnfield realized something was very wrong. He instantly threw his engine into reverse and had time to sound just a short single blast on the whistle, signalling the train crew to apply brakes. But the outcome was inescapable. The wheels of the engine, rotating slowly but inexorably, slipped between the ties — plowing them ahead and tilting the engine over to the right.

END OF THE LINE

The giant smokestack grazed and then fouled the wood lattice on the right side of the structure. What happened next takes far longer to describe than it did to occur. In a matter of a couple of seconds it was over, according to one contemporary account, scarcely sufficient time to say, "May the Lord be merciful!"

This departure announcement, including the 4:10 p.m. train bound for Hamilton, was published in the Hamilton Spectator *a week before the tragedy. For a population unaccustomed to the reliability of railway travel, the advertisement must have promised both punctuality and predictability.*

HAMILTON SPECTATOR, MARCH 5, 1857.

Heeling over to the right, the engine tore out a large section of the wooden side and floor of the bridge, performing a somersault as it slipped into the sharp abyss. Engineer Burnfield and Fireman Knight either jumped or were thrown out as it plunged. Either way, they were carried through the shattering ice by the massive weight of their now-upside-down mount, to sink to the bottom of the canal and instant death. Oxford dragged her tender with her. The leading baggage car, catching the corner of the sinking tender, was thrown to its left, whipsawed down the embankment, and skidded across the ice.

Next followed the leading passenger car, carrying about fifty people. It was this vehicle that sustained the most severe damage and accounted for the greatest loss of life — in fact, only a handful survived its fall. Dragged over the edge of the forty-four-foot abutment, the car had slowed sufficiently to teeter for a fraction of a second before slipping, leading edge down, through the gap in the bridge to the ice below. As it was falling it began to somersault — a movement that accelerated as the front of the car pivoted on the ice. Now upside down, the roof of the carriage smashed into the ice with a sickening thud. The wooden body was crushed and its window glass splintered. By unhappy fate, those who survived the impact were trapped in the darkness of the over-turned vehicle, which had penetrated, but not passed through, the ice. Above them were the unyielding floorboards of the car and beneath them frigid water and slabs of ice.

The second car fared better. The leading end slid over the abutment and grated down its face. The rear truck snagged on the twisted metal of the torn track, slowing the momentum momentarily before it parted from the body. The car ended up almost vertically suspended, with one end crushed on the ice and the other lodged against the stonework of the bridge. But if the car sustained less damage its unhappy occupants still suffered horrendous injuries as they plunged down the height of the upended vehicle accompanied by falling baggage and seats torn from their moorings to land against the still glowing remnants of the stove.

The locomotive, its fire and steam quenched by the freezing water, had vanished from sight. The carriages settled in their precarious position. Sixty souls were dead or dying. The deceased were beyond complaint; the survivors momentarily mute. Over the darkening scene, quietness settled.

CHAPTER TWO

THE NEXT FEW MOMENTS

The silence lasted only a few moments. One contemporary account describes the emergence of "cries and shrieks, groans and obdurations [*sic*] of unearthly intensity." Even given Victorian hyperbole, that can have not been much of an exaggeration. The devastation was truly shocking. Victorian rolling stock was massively, albeit not scientifically, built. The fall of more than forty feet and the impact with the solid surface and the flying debris of seats, stoves, and other equipment resulted in tremendous crushing and cutting injuries. There was immediate peril of drowning and hypothermia, and shock threatened the soaked victims of open cuts and fractures.

Help was not far away. At first it was the numbed survivors, many of them crew members and off-duty employees, who dragged themselves to the aid of their fellow travellers. In fact, a surprising number of railway men experienced dramatic last-second escapes. Perhaps that reflected the sense of ever-looming disaster that characterized Great Western operations. Just-relieved switchman David Crombie was in the best position to save himself. He had placed but a single foot on the very bottom step of the last car before realizing that something was amiss, he had only to drop off and watch helplessly as the train crashed through the bridge. Within a few moments that car leaned precariously against the abutment and he was scurrying to obtain a rope to lower to its shocked occupants.

Before slipping off the train, Crombie was able to call out a warning to those in the last car. William Muir, assistant superintendent on the GWR, was reading in the last seat of that last car. Hearing that cry and feeling the uneven movement of the train, he quickly rose, flung open the rear door, and jumped to safety. Travelling GWR Auditor Richard Jessup, aboard the same car, sensed something wrong and saw conductor Edward Barrett struggling to undo the coupling at the front of the car — or so he thought. The impossibility of such a feat when a train is in motion makes that an unlikely exercise to attempt. In any case Barrett made no claim to such heroics. Standing on the car's front platform he said he heard the brake whistle and someone

Locomotive headlights cast macabre shadows over the disaster scene in this somewhat inaccurate contemporary sketch. The actual bridge latticework was much taller and did not extend beyond the vertical pier.

HAMILTON PUBLIC LIBRARY, LOCAL HISTORY & ARCHIVES, *FRANK LESLIE'S ILLUSTRATED NEWSPAPER*, APRIL 4, 1857.

yell jump — so he did! The example was compelling enough for the auditor. He too jumped, and witnessed the disaster unfolding. Then, wasting no time, Auditor Jessup clambered up the steep side of the embankment and scurried across the high-level suspension bridge. There he begged a ride aboard a passing farm wagon to take him to the terminal where he could raise the alarm.

Edward Sevier, twenty-five-year-old baggageman, in the leading vehicle had an even closer brush with death. Having gathered the Hamilton luggage by the open door he was perched on top of it when he heard the sharp whistle. On looking out he actually claimed to have seen the engine sinking before he too leapt to safety. Forty years later, when he was the only known surviving rail hand to have been on the wreck, he held by his story. In 1897 he told a reporter:

> I saw on looking out of the door the coupling between the tender and (baggage) car break. I saw the engine and tender breaking through the bridge and thinking it was time to get off, I jumped and found myself lying on my back with my head not a foot from the stonework. I saw the engineer throw up his hands as if to jump, but he poor fellow went down with his engine. My chum Henry Urquhart, the express messenger, also went to his death, not being able to get out of the door on the other side of the car.

Traumatic as the experience was, Sevier stayed with the railway long enough to put in twenty-seven years of service and live through several wrecks before retiring to take up the less vicarious life of a letter carrier.

Brakeman Michael Duffey had a similar hair's-breadth escape. He saw Crombie drop-off, heard the whistle, knew that steam had been turned off, and saw "that the engine had gone." In that split-second he jumped and landed just four yards from the edge.

Edwin Richardson, an off-duty conductor, was blissfully asleep in the baggage car. He had no opportunity to react. The first he knew of the disaster was when he was woken by breaking timbers, an explosion of stove ashes, and the onrush of freezing water. That galvanized him into action. Smashing the window, he crawled out onto the ice. There, however, dazed and in pain, he could play no part in the immediate rescue. He recovered sufficiently a little later to try, along with switchman Crombie, to ascertain the cause of the disaster by examining the switch by lamplight.

One of the first non-participants to reach the scene was Diana House, who lived just 100 yards away on the Toronto side, close to the lake. With her sixteen-year-old daughter, she was drawn by the strange sounds emanating from the close-by train and witnessed the drama unfold. Immediately she rushed to the edge of the canal to render what assistance she could. Others shortly joined her.

Although a mile and a half away, the Hamilton station was within sight of the bridge. Whether alerted by Jessup's alarm or the strange activity around the bridge in the failing light, the railway staff was galvanized into action. They formed the vanguard of the hundreds of would-be rescuers and the plain curious who streamed out to the bridge, along the line, and across the ice. The proximity of GWR workshops and yards made it possible to respond quickly with heavy equipment. Special trains were marshalled: first to carry apparatus, later to transport the dead and injured. Ropes and ladders were positioned to help rescuers and wounded scramble up and down the steep banks of the canal. The militia was called in. Major Alfred Booker Junior (whose father, Alfred Senior, the hell-fire preacher, was among the victims) stationed his company of troops at the depot to restore order and deter looters. Captain Macdonald's Rifles were marched to the disaster scene to provide assistance.

Recovery efforts continued through the night and the following day. It was bitterly cold, but thankfully moonlit. Locomotive headlights were rigged at the scene — casting both helpful light and eerie shadow. At first, efforts were directed toward releasing those trapped in the near-vertical second car, perilously inclined against the abutment.

One of those extracted from that last car was a Woodstock dry-goods merchant by the name of W.R. Marshall, who was seated four seats from the back. He was alerted by the "oscillation of the car" and the mounting alarm displayed by the crew and his fellow travellers. A take-charge type of person and unaware of the proximity of the bridge, Marshall stayed put and calmly advised others to do the same. Given the providential escapes of those who jumped that was clearly rather dubious advice — but there is no evidence that anyone heeded his poor counsel. Marshall grimly rode down with the last car. When the front of it smashed into the rock-hard surface of the frozen canal, seats, fittings, hand luggage, and occupants were torn from their places to lodge in a sickening mass of humanity, wood, and iron at the partly submerged front-end of the car. Here, in total darkness, Marshall found himself crushed "almost to suffocation." With blood oozing from his mouth and fearing that his next breath must be his last, he can perhaps be forgiven for his theatrical reconstruction of his circumstances.

> The next few moments were the worst I ever witnessed: oh that it may never be my lot to experience the like again. Some prayed, others called upon the saints, others swore fearful oaths, and all seemed writhing in the deepest agony. I can only liken the place to a slaughterhouse. The blood streamed down over my face and clothes as if some huge beast had been slain above me.

Further in his recorded recollections, the saintly Marshall waxed even more melodramatic.

> What an awful lesson does this shocking event teach those who habitually put off making their peace

with God to some future day, or to a death bed. The writer of these few lines will consider himself amply repaid, if his description succeeds in persuading one sinner to seek a refuge in Him who promised to be a present help unto his people in every time of trial.

Hopefully, the upstanding Mr. Marshall maintained such commendable thoughts over the ten minutes or so before he was rescued. His own recollection is that he spent the time enjoining his fellow victims to be patient and wait for help. His reminiscences adopted a rather tetchy tone, however, in describing his actual release — as if a little resentful of the intrusion into his virtuous soliloquy! First, the top of the car was smashed in, providing welcome light and air. Then, almost immediately, Marshall recalls his temple being grazed by a near glance from a well-intentioned crowbar. Not willing to be placed a second time in jeopardy of meeting his maker, he made a monumental effort to seize the instrument. Immediately a hand (which curiously he judged to be a woman's hand) reached in and was clasped over his mouth, threatening, yet again, to suffocate him. Once more he made a mighty effort and dislodged the hand. Whether his would-be rescuer was so discouraged by all this resistance or whether the good Mr. Marshall simply took matters into his own hand, the balance of his escape he ascribes to his own initiative — at least up to the point where, having dragged himself out of the car and to the edge of the canal, he was hauled by chains to the top of the bank. From there he was carried to a nearby switchman's hut and given medical attention. His condition immediately after the event was curiously described as "severely though not dangerously wounded." He was without more ado taken to his brother-in-law's residence not far away on Queen Street, where he recuperated.

Perhaps Marshall's counsel to his fellow travellers that they remain seated was not entirely without merit. Although those who jumped were saved, at least one survivor believed that the failed effort to reach the door might have cost some their lives. W.W. Reed was seated in the fourth seat of the last car on the left-hand side. At the very front on that side, with his feet on the stove, sat Mr. H.M. Yerrington. Behind him was Samuel Zimmerman and behind him another wealthy contractor, Mr. Farr. When derailment appeared likely, Reed, who had been reading a newspaper, simply braced himself in his seat. He saw Farr and Zimmerman dash past him, making for the rear door, which they almost reached. When the car toppled, however, Farr and Zimmerman fell nearly the entire length of the car to be wedged up against the stove in all the rubble. Yerrington, already seated in front of the stove, collapsed on top of them — Farr and Zimmerman providing human insulation from the scorching heat. When he was extricated, Yerrington was soaked in blood, and therefore reported as in critical condition. By the following day, however, he was sufficiently recovered from his modest injuries to be going out for a walk. The blood, undoubtedly, was from his

The scene at ice level was frantic and determined. Armed with only a few ineffective tools, rescuers tried desperately to break through the massive frames of the cars while others shone bright lanterns or attempted rudimentary first-aid.

HAMILTON PUBLIC LIBRARY, LOCAL HISTORY & ARCHIVES, *FRANK LESLIE'S ILLUSTRATED NEWSPAPER*, APRIL 4, 1857.

now-dead companions, who, in Reed's opinion, might have survived had they stayed seated. Yerrington, on the other hand, seated in front of the stove, might have been the one to be crushed against it.

How much of the second car penetrated the ice is not known, but it certainly broke through. When Zimmerman's body was eventually recovered it showed clear evidence of having been submerged for some hours. Yet, initially the stove situated in front of the first seats was at least partially above water. In the darkness, Reed could hear the anguished cries of a woman below him who was being burned to death. This raised the spectre of the too-common consequences of nineteenth century wrecks: fire. It occupied Reed's thoughts for a time as he waited for the seemingly inevitable conflagration. Whether only the first few feet of the car were underwater (sufficient to account for the waterlogged bodies) or whether it settled further during the first few minutes, enough to extinguish the stove, is not known.

The story of another survivor, John Smith of Michigan, confirms that the last car penetrated the ice. He was seated on the right-hand side (opposite where the stove was located) in the third seat from the front. Like some of the others he made a dash for the door when he realized something was badly amiss. (The frantic rush to "abandon ship" perhaps says something of the lack of confidence GWR passengers of the era felt, as well as the often sluggish pace of travel that could make such an option possible.) Smith never made it to the door, but as the car began to slip he managed to grab hold of a hook and only lost control at the bottom of the plunge, when he found himself submersed in water. Only after swallowing a good deal was he able to twist his face sufficiently to breathe. Nearby, beneath the water, he could feel the head of an already dead victim. Bruised, cut, and suffering from hypothermia, Smith was eventually transported to the Anglo American Hotel, where it was many hours before he could stop shivering.

Of those in the first car only a handful survived, and those who did essentially extricated themselves from the wreckage. William Garrick, yet another Great Western employee, was seated four or five seats from the front of the ill-fated car, on the left-hand side. When the whistle blew and the train gave two sharp jerks he rose to his feet. Out of one of the front windows on the opposite side he could see the end of the masonry parapet appear. Unbeknownst to him the engine must already have been well on the way to its icy resting place, and the baggage car was flying across the gap. However, at the time he assumed that the engine must have been near the end of the bridge. As the car canted down he resumed his seat and held on while it somersaulted head-over-heels to the frozen canal. When he told his story to the Coroner's Inquest, he matter-of-factly described finding himself in the frigid waters and crawling out "not much hurt."

But it was not his near miraculous escape from so deadly a calamity that interested the jurors. By yet another of those quirks that dog this tale, Garrick was actually a carpenter employed by the railway on bridge and culvert repair. In fact, he had been repair foreman on the Desjardins Canal Bridge. The previous August he had supervised the placement of an additional twelve needle beams (beams that support the track in a similar manner to railway ties) to provide greater strength to the structure. Only a few months before the accident, he had been in charge of replacing seventeen broken and chipped beams in the same part that collapsed the night of the tragedy. The restoration had been made necessary by an earlier incident in which a freight car had derailed on the bridge.

The salvation of one of the few other survivors of the first car was touched with great tragedy. John Clare, a Hamilton merchant, seemed oblivious to impending disaster until the car actually began its decent. Next thing he knew he was trapped under the weight of the heavy stove, badly cut. He made no complaint of burns, so either the freezing water had quenched the fire or he was quickly able to extricate himself. With great difficulty he pulled himself from the middle of the upturned and partially submerged vehicle to a broken window at one end, which he crawled through onto the ice. He was quite certain that if anyone else availed themselves of the same exit it was not after he had done so — for he would not be budged from the spot. Only with great reluctance was he eventually enticed away to warmth and safety, but he did so without his two-year-old daughter, Mahaly, whom at the time of the accident was perched upon his knee. Her remains were recovered the following day.

If possible, the story of the Doyle family is even more tragic. At least seven of the Pickering, Ontario, area family were travelling in the leading car: Timothy, a shoemaker, his wife, Ann, and their three young children. Also in the party were Timothy's brothers Patrick and Owen. Some early reports added two cousins, a cousin's wife, and two of their daughters to the group. If so, the extended Doyle family would have accounted for about one-quarter of the travellers in the ill-fated first car. Mention of the cousins was dropped from later accounts, so most likely they were simply a manifestation of the immediate confusion.

What is certain is that Timothy and his wife perished, as did his two-year-old son, also called Timothy, along with one of his brothers. Timothy's other brother, Owen, survived by breaking through a window and half swimming, half crawling onto the ice, before losing consciousness. Somehow or other he was able to push his eight-year-old niece ahead of him and to drag her nine-year-old brother to the window. As Diana House, the nearby resident, stumbled and rolled down the steep and frozen bank she came across the girl who, it is said, pleaded: "Oh, don't mind me, save my brother." House could see the boy grimly clutching the window frame, with his chin barely above water. She could hear his desperate cries for help. Although the ice had fractured around the almost submerged car, she was able to reach the boy and drag him to safety. Clutching the freezing lad, she enlisted the aid of a passenger, himself badly injured, to carry the girl on his back. Together they hurried the children to her home, where she bundled them into bed. Apparently, by morning, the two exhibited no physical effects from their experience. But they surely could never have overcome the psychological trauma of the accident and the loss of so many of their loved ones.

The equipment rushed from Hamilton had made recovery efforts on the near-vertical second car relatively quick and easy. All the bodies, living or dead, were concentrated at what had been the front of the cars. It was a relatively simple matter to force entry (although not completely without incident, as the upright Mr. Marshall's brush with the crowbar demonstrated). Salvage efforts on the leading car were largely limited to recovering bodies, complicated by the need to break through the sturdy floorboards to gain entry, and because there was no way of telling where in the length of the car victims might be found.

As the night wore on less delicate means were adopted. Men on makeshift rafts probed the nine-foot depths of the canal (now a patchwork of fractured ice and frigid murky water) with long poles, testing for the resiliency that would signal a body. All night the efforts continued. Attempts to raise the first passenger car were hampered by the still-perilously placed second car, so with the aid of axes and saws the latter was dismantled and dragged to the shore. Heavy tackle was mounted on each abutment and, although they were able to raise the leading car a bit, it too had to be demolished the following day.

Brute force and rudimentary equipment were all that the rescuers could marshal in the salvage effort. How much they accomplished, under circumstances that would have to be considered extreme even by today's well-equipped and trained professional rescue crews, is amazing. In deep water, at temperatures cold enough to kill, with only locomotive headlights and moonlight to provide illumination and at risk of being crushed by the precariously balanced car and doubtful bridge, teams of impromptu volunteers managed to save the living, recover most of the bodies, and clear much of the debris.

Their accomplishments speak to their resolve and tenacity. Amidst the general vigour some examples of individual heroism stand out — perhaps none more so than that of one man, who caught the eye of a reporter for the *Hamilton Spectator*. "Who," he asked, "is that noble fellow who early at the scene worked like a second Hercules unceasingly for hours hewing away at the timbers of the cars, in his shirt sleeves, and up to his waist in water?" The image caught the imagination of the public and for a day or two the identity of "That Noble Fellow" was on many peoples' minds. The *Spectator* was able to put a name to the hero when a correspondent reported him to be Alexander Middlemis, a GWR carpenter. "He was lifted from the water," the letter-writer observed, "after two hours exertion covered over with ice." The correspondent added a second name, George Bourne, another railway carpenter, who took over from Middlemis and worked like another Hercules. Like a super abundance of shopping-mall Santas, the list of claimant "Hercules" began to grow. A day or two later, the *Spectator* commented: "Two other persons have put in claims to the distinction assigned Alexander Middlemis as the noble hearted fellow who was conspicuously the observed of all observers in rescuing the dead and dying from the ill-fated train at the Bridge, on the night of the 12th instant." That torturous sentence, perhaps, revealed the waning interest of the reporter in the matter. He went on to identify the first of the newly identified as John A. McGillis, and then with commendable honesty continued: "The name of the other we have forgotten." The proximity of the accident scene to GWR maintenance shops meant that, in fact, many employees played heroically key roles in the rescue. Although "That Noble Fellow" may have stood out, many of his colleagues demonstrated selfless exertions that night. The minute books of the Great Western are notably terse on the subject of the accident, but they do include an expression of thanks to those many employees.

Within a few hours treating the wounded and comforting the survivors gave way to collecting and transporting the dead, many of whom had initially been laid out on the ice and foreshore. By all accounts this was conducted in a most businesslike manner. Flatcars and barrows were used to bring most of them to the baggage and freight rooms at the station. There they were laid out in an orderly fashion in rows, each with a chalked number marked on the floor at their feet. Coroners Bull and Rosebrugh supervised the process and, at first, strictly limited access to the buildings. Many mourners, in fact, had to wait until the Friday before even being permitted to view the dead. There were reasons for the tight security. Not only were many of the victims carrying considerable wealth but there was also a crush of anxious relatives and friends, a good many of whom had been waiting at the station since before the accident. The coroners held their ground and Alfred Booker's Artillery Brigade enforced order. They did not entirely avoid unpleasantness. At least one attempt to steal from the corpses was curtailed by the ruffian being felled by a stunning blow delivered by a GWR mechanic. The perpetrator was taken into custody. Someone managed to purloin a travelling bag belonging to Samuel Zimmerman — specially crafted to contain a set of monogrammed silver toilet items. Zimmerman had purchased it in Paris at a cost of around five hundred dollars.

An account in the *Toronto Globe* describes the general appearance of the victims as ghastly. "The general expression on the countenance was that of fear and alarm; the eyeballs stretched to the utmost, the mouth open, and the hands generally fixed in an attitude of defense." At the instruction of the Managing Director of the Great Western C.J. Brydges, a local photographer, R. Milne, was hired to take photographic images of the deceased to assist in

This contemporary sketch captured the grim setting in the Great Western's baggage rooms. In the shadowy light, bodies were arrayed in orderly rows, guarded by the militia and surrounded by an anxious crowd of relatives.

HAMILTON PUBLIC LIBRARY, LOCAL HISTORY & ARCHIVES, *FRANK LESLIE'S ILLUSTRATED NEWSPAPER*, APRIL 4, 1857.

later identification. He employed a "force of artisans" equipped with "several sets of apparatus." This was a novel concept and is believed to have been the first such use of photography.

The scene was grim. Security was tight. When the grieving were allowed in there were numerous anguished episodes. It was still an era when ladies were expected to swoon. The gloom, the watchful militia glowering in the shadows, the cold, and the wretched condition of the dead must have created a horrible pastiche.

Virtually every member of the community was affected — whether personally touched by grief, directly involved in the frantic rescue efforts, or simply caught-up in the electric atmosphere that charged the usually tranquil night with unusual activity. Eleanor Bull, a young pastor's wife about to give birth to her first child, was unable to sleep due to the constant tramp of horses and wagons on the Caledonia Plank Road that passed their cottage. Not until the morning was she told of the significance of the strange nighttime movements.

All that night the post office and telegraph offices remained open, handling the spate of outgoing dispatches and the flurry of incoming messages seeking confirmation and reassurance. The *Spectator* began publishing special edition after special edition in order to keep up with the demand. Newsboys flooded the city with the extras. Over the next day 6,000 copies were consigned to New York destined for Britain via the steamship *Persia*. The usual two bags could hold only one half of the sudden rush of mail destined for Britain. So dramatically had communications changed over the preceding decade that shortly after the Legislative Assembly in Toronto (Canada's pre-Confederation Parliament rotated between Toronto and Quebec City) reassembled at 7:30 p.m. that very evening, rumours of the catastrophe began to circulate. Among those reported dead were Zimmerman and two members of Parliament.

Shortly, a newspaper extra was brought into the house with sufficient confirmation that, at the urging of the opposition, the house was adjourned. In assenting, on behalf of the government, John A. Macdonald, then the attorney general, observed that he had reason to fear that gentlemen well-known to the house and of great worth and merit had met with their death by that lamentable accident; and he quite concurred that the house was not in a position to go on with its business.

CHAPTER THREE

The Day Dawned Clear

Mercifully, overnight the temperature crept up toward the freezing mark for the first time that entire month. By 9:00 a.m. the thermometer had nudged just past 0° Celsius (33° Fahrenheit) and as on the previous day the sky was clear — the sun having eroded most of the remaining snow on surrounding hillsides.

In the morning, school children played hooky to visit the grim site. Many years later, Thomas Kilvington remembered being strictly forbidden from visiting the gruesome wreck. Along with other curious classmates, he disobeyed the admonition and hiked the long trip from his home only to immediately encounter his father among the assembled throng!

The view that greeted them was quite different from what it had been the previous night. The near-vertical second car had been dragged down, broken up, and moved aside. Although many "photographic" records of the site taken in daylight show that car still in place, closer examination reveals that the artists had taken licence in trying to illustrate the scene by adding back in the missing detail. Winches had been set up on the two abutments, but attempts to raise the first, practically submerged car were stymied by a section of the bridge that had collapsed on top of it. At daybreak they were finally successful in budging the debris and gaining full access to the car. Some fifteen to twenty bodies were then recovered. Although, at that point, most of the victims had, in fact, been accounted for, it was believed at the time that perhaps another twenty had slipped beneath the ice. What remained of the first car was demolished and efforts to locate the casualties continued. Among the last to be brought to the surface was George Knight the eighteen-year-old fireman from Windsor, Ontario.

After the last wave of victims from the leading car had been accommodated, the pressure on those engaged in the temporary mortuaries began to slacken. Toward the end of the day after the disaster, most of the bodies had been identified and some had been removed to local residences or dispatched to their hometowns. The firebrand rebel William Lyon Mackenzie claimed that even in this process, the Great Western had been so insensitive as to levy a charge of four dollars for the crude box provided to transport each victims' remains. Mackenzie, no lover of either the political

In 1857 photography was usually limited to controlled indoor lighting and lengthy exposures, but this salt-paper print by an unknown photographer was captured for perpetuity the morning after the disaster, looking towards Burlington Bay.
LIBRARY AND ARCHIVES CANADA, MIKAN 3203866.

establishment or railways in general, may well have been guilty of broadcasting unfounded gossip — the more likely, since this accusation does not appear to have been levelled elsewhere. Still, it was this sort of writing that generated readership for Mackenzie's *Weekly Record*, the radical press of its time.

This 1850s photograph of William Lyon Mackenzie oozes irascibility. The one-time rebel and lifelong reformer was also a dedicated adversary of Sir Alan MacNab, of the Great Western, and of just about anything to do with capitalism.

NIAGARA FALLS PUBLIC LIBRARY, D422259.

With community hysteria starting to subside and the immediate strain on authorities beginning to slacken, the machine of law and process was put in motion. The coroners retired to the nearby boardroom of the Great Western and empanelled a jury to examine the circumstances surrounding the unnatural deaths of the victims. They then immediately adjourned the inquest to the following day, Saturday.

Even before the jury was struck, the morning after the accident Hamilton City Council was convened to express "heartfelt sympathy to the suffers and friends of the deceased." They then went on to resolve:

> That in humble submission to the Providence of Him, without whom not a sparrow falleth to the ground, but whose inscrutable wisdom permitted this City to be visited by a fearful calamity on the Great Western Railroad, by which some of our most respected friends and citizens have been hurried into eternity, be it therefore resolved that the inhabitants of this City be respectfully required to set apart Monday 16th March as a day of humiliation: they are requested to cease from the ordinary occupations of the week and meet in their respective congregations on that day, and that the proclamation of his Worship be issued to that effect.

While order was being slowly restored, the salvage effort continued. For the second night, workers carried on removing the debris and dragging the canal under the glow of the locomotive headlights and the flicker of myriad bonfires. That night one new resident of Dundas, Britton Osler, who lived three or more miles away at the head of the valley, breathlessly wrote to his brother Featherstone detailing the events and adding: "We can see out of the window now the lights of the bridge where they are yet fishing out the dead." Perhaps a reflection of his upbringing (his father was the newly appointed Anglican rector to Dundas and Ancaster) he provided the rather unusual headcount of the dead: "4 clergymen, 1 Church of England." Somewhat luridly, and inaccurately, he wrote: "Mr. Zimmerman of Niagara Falls was among the first to be taken out with his head completely off." Young Osler, then only eighteen years old, may be forgiven his youthful insensitivity. The letter penned by his mother, Ellen, in Toronto, to his brother earlier in the day had a vastly different timbre. That letter practically screams of a mother's anxiety and distress.

The family was in the midst of relocating from Bond Head, north of Toronto, to Dundas where the Reverend Featherstone Osler Senior was hoping to provide a better education for his family. The move involving a large family was complex. Two sons, including Britton, travelled ahead, as did their father. One son at least, the younger Featherstone, was to stay in Bond Head for the time being. Their mother, accompanied by younger members of the family, was making the journey that fateful week. That trip was interrupted when eight-year-old William came down with the croup. That necessitated a stay in a Toronto hotel. Two family members then proceeded alone, taking the train immediately preceding the wreck. Britton, undoubtedly on the way to meet that train, wrote to his brother of seeing it cross the Desjardins Canal Bridge from the carriage bridge, above.

Even a century and a half later, Ellen's letter to Featherstone, hastily scrawled across three pages, still betrays a mother's distress that her son would be worried about their welfare, as well as her own trepidation when it had seemed possible that the advance party might have been on board: "Martha and John went up yesterday and for some time I thought they must have been passengers on the cars that were lost but they fortunately left by the mid-day train." She only received assurance of their safety when her husband telegraphed her the same day she wrote the letter, the day after the disaster. Having gasped-out the happy tidings of their safety she reverts with mild incongruity to her role as mother. The very next sentence reads: "Poor Martha had the fits again and what to do with her I know not."

This 1867 image shows Britton Bath Osler as a dignified legal expert and future prosecutor of Louis Riel. A decade earlier, the scribbled letter to his father, written when the tragic details at Desjardins were beginning to circulate, reveals a more callow youth, preoccupied the grisly details and body counts.

MCCORD MUSEUM, I-27210.1.

The story of the Osler's brush with death illustrates the vagaries of fate. Although none were on board, the family's itinerary seems to have been woven around the tragedy. As with any who just miss or just manage to board a ship, plane, or train destined for disaster, personal lives and history might have had to be rewritten had fate been different.

Young William might well have been aboard and killed. If so, one of the most celebrated Canadian doctors of the time might have never enjoyed his career. William Osler went on to become chief of medicine at Johns Hopkins and a professor of medicine at both Oxford and McGill universities. The youthfully insensitive Britton served as one of the crown prosecutors at the trial of Louis Reil and, curiously, became one of the most prominent railway lawyers of his time. His knowledge of engineering detail became so advanced that he was made an associate of the Canadian Society of Civil Engineers. The younger Featherstone later became a respected judge in the Ontario Court of Appeal. The family somehow skirted the disaster to contribute separate chapters to the country's story.

In Hamilton that Saturday morning, a day and a half after the calamity, arrangements for funeral services and burials were being made. Although funeral homes were just starting to provide embalming and dressing services, the norm was still for the funeral procession to start from the residence of the deceased or from a relative or friend's home. After the funeral service, held in a place of worship, the departed were taken to the cemetery.

The more severe winters experienced in the nineteenth century, combined with the rudimentary tools then available to gravediggers, constituted something of a problem. Given that the ice in the canal was reported to be two-feet thick, it is clear that the ground would have been hard frozen. Interment in family vaults was straightforward: the capstone had only to be lifted and the casket carried down to be sealed in its niche. Some gravesites were prepared ahead of time, in milder weather, doubtless discomforting should the intended occupant become aware of the preparations.

For the most part, however, winter burials were simply accommodated in communal vaults until the ground was sufficiently thawed. In the Hamilton cemetery such a storage vault, now abandoned, is built deep into the side of the escarpment. The mind easily conjures macabre images of the frenetic haste that must have occurred each spring as cemetery workers wallowed in the wet, malodorous earth to dig graves of sufficient depth. Every increased degree of warmth that made their job easier only increased the urgency of completing their task before the warmth penetrated the stacked coffins deep in the hillside.

Register, Thermometer, Barometer &c., Hamilton, 1857.					
	THERMOMETER.		BAROMETER.		WEATHER:
DATE.	9¼ A.M.	9, P.M.	9, A.M.	9, P.M.	
March 1.	20°	20°	29.22	29.42	Snowing all day.
2...	2	8	.34	.81	Fair and clear; sleighing.
3...	12	27	.62	.47	Mostly cloudy.
4...	28	22	.56	.57	Fair and clear; sleighing gone.
5...	38	35	.85	.80	Partly cloudy; a little snow in the morning.
6.....	23	18	.87	.48	Fair and clear
7...	18	15	.70	.82	Mostly cloudy.
8...	17	23	.93	.68	Fair and clear; evening cloudy.
9...	25	15	.27	.55	Snowing; heavily in the morning; sleighing.
10...	10	18	.68	.60	Fair and clear.
11...	16	22	.56	.66	Partly cloudy; snow shower in the evening.
12.....	14	17	.66	.95	Fair and clear; sleighing gone
13....	21	20	.90	.66	Do do.
14....	33	33	.52	.65	Partly cloudy.
15....	30	32	.72	.62	Fair and clear.
16....	33	35	.50	.50	Partly cloudy. Slight snow showers.
17....	35	36	.66	.63	Fair and clear.
18....	37	42	.42	.40	Cloudy; some rain a. m. and p. m.
19.....	33	32	.35	.38	Snowing moderately all day.
20....	33	37	.51	.45	Fair and clear.
21....	38	40	.46	.82	Do do.
22....	42	37	30.00	.84	Clear a. m. cloudy p. m.
23....	35	44	29.47	.70	Partly cloudy, windy.
24....	36	40	.87	.50	Do do.
25.....	35	38	.50	.60	Do do.
26....	33	35	.67	.68	Fair and clear.
27....	34	35	.65	.62	Partly cloudy.
28....	26.	35	.68	.70	Do do.
29....	40	35	.76	.83	Fair and clear.
30....	41	39	.93	.87	Do do.
31....	42	47	.85	.47	Do do. evening cloudy.
Means	28.27	30.9	29.616	29.62	Highest, 62°; lowest, -2°
Mean temperature of the month, 29.986°					Average of 11 preceding years, 28.82°.

The weather register for Hamilton in March 1857 shows the conditions that prevailed around the date of the wreck. On the day of the disaster the thermometer hovered well below 0°Celsius. In contrast to conditions a day or two earlier, the notation on the day of the accident read "sleighing gone."

HAMILTON SPECTATOR, APRIL 7, 1857.

The prominence of many of the victims resulted in some truly impressive displays of sombre respect. Among the first funerals to be held was that of the Reverend Theodore Heise, whose disfigured remains were escorted by an ecumenical bevy of clergy and a procession of native Germans along with their wives and children, who formed his congregation. Another interment that Saturday was John Sharpe, the partially crippled, half-blind keeper of a bookstall at the Hamilton station.

Sunday morning the churches were packed to capacity. Congregations eschewed finery and the pulpits altars and galleries were draped in black. The music selected and the sermons reflected the despondence of the flock, and the services were interrupted by occasional stifled cries.

In the afternoon the funerals recommenced. Alexander Burnfield, the twenty-nine-year-old locomotive engineer, was carried into the Hamilton Cemetery (then frequently referred to as the Burlington Cemetery). At the head of the procession was the Great Western's Locomotive superintendent, accompanied by the foremen from the Toronto and Hamilton shops and several hundred of Burnfield's fellow employees. His grave, apparently, was ready to receive him. The reporter from the *Hamilton Spectator* described the gravediggers, begrimed with the evidence of their trade, as barely having completed their work before the funeral party arrived. An eloquent graveside service was reportedly listened to attentively before the Scottish-born Burnfield was committed to the ground to be grieved by his widow and young family.

The cortèges of John Henderson and Mrs. P.S. Stevenson (wife of the sherriff) were formed in a single procession for the journey to the cemetery. Following the single hearse were more than a hundred carriages and a great many mourners on foot. Henderson was the brother-in-law of C.J. Brydges, managing director of the Great Western, a respected astronomer, a telegraphic engineer, and a former employee of the railway. The Great Western was represented by a number of officials, several directors, and a great number of workers who had met the oncoming procession after departing from Burnfield's interment. Also present were the mayor and a number of councilors.

The ceremonies for former-city counselor Donald Stuart were held at St. Mary's Church. So packed was it that thousands were unable to gain access. Scarcely had Stuart's coffin been dispatched to the Catholic cemetery than its place was taken by two: those of the sisters Ellen and Mary Devine. A short ceremony was conducted and they too were on the way to the cemetery.

After a funeral service in the Park Street Baptist Church the remains of the Reverend Alfred Booker were taken to the cemetery in a procession sixty carriages long followed by a crowd on foot. Heading the procession was his son Major Booker — the same who several years earlier marched at the head of the triumphal parade inaugurating Great Western service to Hamilton and had also marshalled his force at the disaster scene to impose order. Now leading a double column of his Artillery Company, dressed in plainclothes with crepe armbands, he paid his last tributes to his stern father. The militia formed-up at the entrance, providing a lane down which passed the hearse and nearly every clergyman in the city.

All that Sunday the city was preoccupied with grieving. The church bells rang first for the Sabbath services then with the mournful tolling for the succession of funerals.

If it were possible, Monday was an even more sombre day. That was the day the council had declared as a "day of public humiliation." Normal business activities were suspended, flags flew at half-mast, and divine services were held in all the churches both morning and afternoon. Two funeral cortèges met at the corner of York and MacNab streets — a short distance from the cemetery gates. They were those of popular marine captain James Sutherland, and the young barrister and son of Hamilton's first mayor, Adam Ferrie Junior. Combined, the two funerals exceeded the seemingly endless length of the previous day's processions. No less than 140 carriages joined in the journey to the cemetery. Leading the procession were the mayor and the Corporation of Hamilton along with the police force. Sutherland's casket was draped in the Union Jack and carried on an open cart. Immense numbers attended the ceremonies at the burial ground. Among the monuments marking the graves of other members of his prominent family a broken stone column surmounted by a carved wreath still stands over Adam Ferrie's resting place. The break in the column is deliberate — intended to recognize a life cut short. Adam Ferrie was just twenty-four years old.

While Hamilton was going about the ceremonial business of burying its dead, Clifton (now part of Niagara Falls, Ontario) was organizing a funeral extravaganza for its most flamboyant citizen, Samuel Zimmerman. If the newspaper reports are even half correct the Zimmerman funeral was the most spectacular witnessed in this country and may not have been eclipsed yet. As well as being an exceptionally prominent and well-connected financier and a generous philanthropist, Zimmerman was an active Freemason and his funeral was to be conducted with the full rites of that organization.

The following report in the *Spectator* was widely reprinted throughout southern Ontario:

> On Monday morning, March 16th a numerous band proceeded to the cars on their way to Niagara Falls, his late residence. A crowd of brethren swelled the throng at every station along the road. At the bridge, those from the United States joined the sad array. Their cars were festooned with curtains of lustrous white and sombre black sustained and fixed by large rosettes between the alternate windows. Their locomotive was also similarly covered, and black crepe muffled its sounding bell. The Erie and Ontario road was opened especially for the occasion, and a long train of cars passed more than once between the stations, at the bridge and at the Falls, freighted with a host of masons.
>
> At the Clifton House, the large assembly met, and filled the great hall close by. There were the

> powerful contractor and the poor day labourer, the merchant prince and the humble clerk, the man of boundless acres and the backwoodsman, eminent members of the legislature, the press, the bar, and all other professions. There was the centarian, gray with years, the youth just budding into manhood, and the "Lewis" the scion of a Masonic race. There was the venerable High Priest in his long white robe, with the golden mitre upon his head and the golden breast plate upon his bosom.

The assembly climbed the hill to the Zimmerman residence on the escarpment, where the body lay, and there formed a funeral procession of extraordinary dimensions. Every rank of the Masonic Order was represented. The cortège contained two bands, one from Rochester, New York, and the other from Buffalo. Among the mourners were two of Zimmerman's brothers, his children, his first father-in-law, and the receiver general of the country, J. Morrison. Among the friends were several members of the legislature and the mayors of St. Catharines, Niagara, and Buffalo. Among the Masonic lodges represented were those from New York City, Buffalo, Milwaukee, Syracuse, and Rochester, and from the states of Ohio, Michigan, Illinois, and Pennsylvania. Canadian representatives came from Montreal, London, Toronto, Hamilton, and other cities.

In all, some ten thousand persons marched in the procession or witnessed the ceremonies from nearby hillsides and buildings. After the reading of the Church of England burial service the Masonic rituals were observed. Finally, the body was laid to rest in a temporary vault set in the hillside surrounded by the ornamental gardens and commanding a panoramic and uninterrupted view of the American and Horseshoe Falls.

CHAPTER FOUR

One Bold Operator

Of those who died in the accident, without a doubt the most celebrated was Samuel Zimmerman. Newspaper reports described him as either the first- or second-richest man in the country. As his executors began the task of unravelling his estate that estimate underwent very substantial revision. Apparently he had learned how to put other people's money to work in his own interest. Nevertheless, Zimmerman undoubtedly had a greater degree of political, financial, and social influence than anyone since. Zimmerman is a true Canadian enigma, whose role in history has been essentially obscured.

Following his death a curious riches-to-rags saga played out. On his passing his holdings were liquidated, his partially completed mansion abandoned, and his memory virtually expunged. One can search among the numerous memorials that dot the public parks of Niagara Falls, the city Zimmerman did so much to create, and will find no marker to commemorate his life. One glorious remnant of the formal gardens he created — a fountain that cost $15,000 to erect in the 1850s — endured for about a century. Then it was decapitated, and today is nothing more than a shallow goldfish pond fed by a few ugly utilitarian nozzles. As many as ten thousand people attended his funeral, but the temporary hillside vault in which he was laid to rest, commanding a panoramic view of both the American and Horseshoe Falls, remained in place just a few short years. In order to accommodate the forced sale of his estate it was dismantled, and Zimmerman's remains were shipped to the outskirts of the city to be reinterred within the vault he had built for his first wife.

Even then his ignominy was not complete. His massive casket was too large to enter the burial crypt. Before it would fit, the outer casket was removed and the lead lining peeled off and sold to a local scrap dealer. There was even a rumour that the metal ended up being recycled into pipes for the Niagara water supply! For more than a century his new resting place remained unmemorialized, until the local historical society commissioned a mason to chisel a few details into the back of his first wife's headstone.

Who was Samuel Zimmerman and what role did he play in mid-nineteenth century Canada? Modern phrases tend to give somewhat distorted impressions. A "Who's Who" of the 1850s would probably have described him as a "railway contractor." Yet, while he had direct

Samuel Zimmerman was aptly described as "one bold operator." His various guises included contractor, financier, manipulator, showman, philanthropist, and scamp. Although aggressive and astute, Sam lived life on a grand scale and knew how to temper the hard edge of business with extravagant hospitality.

NIAGARA FALLS PUBLIC LIBRARY, D10559.

responsibility for the construction of many hundreds of miles of railway, he routinely subcontracted the work and took none of the pride of a job well done that characterized the great civil engineering firms of the period. Today we might describe him as a political lobbyist, par excellence. But that label is far too superficial to cover the range of Zimmerman's activities. In the decade or so before his death he had become as influential in the corridors of power as many of the leading lawmakers themselves. This complex man, with the ability to beguile politicians and dictate policies, had absolutely no interest in seeking public office. Instead he relished in parlaying his influence into financial gain and personal prestige.

In light of his activities, Zimmerman could perhaps best be described as a thoroughly corrupt and greedy capitalist. Indeed, if he were operating in today's world that would be a very accurate characterization. But the business environment in late-colonial Canada was altogether different from today's regulated regime, with its insistence on the separation of political and private interests.

Before his untimely death, Zimmerman had finished the four gatehouses, the ornamental gardens, and the actual footings of his planned mansion facing the American Falls at Niagara. The gatehouses and stables were built of imported yellow English brick. The stables alone (pictured above) cost $18,000 and lasted until the 1950s, when they were destroyed to permit construction of the present-day Comfort Inn.

NIAGARA FALLS PUBLIC LIBRARY, D415590.

Politics were the preserve of the wealthy and wealth was the reward of politics. In an era when a voice in government was limited to only proppertied men, nothing different could be expected. With a sense of noblesse oblige they clung to the same presumptions that would later be manifest in the American business adage: "What is good for General Motors is good for the country." Most Victorian politicians enjoyed a happy symbiosis between their commercial and legislative responsibilities. Indeed, the erstwhile chairman of the Great Western Railway, Sir Allan MacNab, continued to hold a directorship in the line while acting as chairman of the Railway Committee of the legislature. Even while serving as Canadian premier, MacNab continued to openly act in the company's interests — especially where they coincided with his own.

Many a corrupt man has argued that he was not being any more unscrupulous than anyone else. Certainly many of those whom Zimmerman swindled were players in the same game. Zimmerman stood out simply as a man who played the game better than others! That is not to condone or excuse his perfidy. However, the times were not so corrupt that no one publicly decried the collusion. After all, the victims were not all well-heeled punters. Public money was massively diverted to subsidize railway building and promoters often extorted municipal subscriptions through the simple threat of bypassing a town. These funds were the ones that the promoters, contractors, and legislators divvied up among themselves with such bonhomie. The phrase "railway morality" was coined to describe the unsavoury ethics that distinguished the transportation politics of the day — and this was decades before John A. Macdonald's government became embroiled in the Pacific Scandal, during the building of the CPR, that so corroded the reputation of post-Confederation Parliament.

Zimmerman could easily be passed off as a venial, conniving miser, but nothing could be further from the truth. Those who knew him found him affable and generous — a philanthropist and a bon vivant. His magical influence was achieved not through coercion so much as persuasion; not by extortion but by subtle gifts and bribes. He also knew well how to "work to contract." The celebrated Canadian civil engineer Thomas Keefer, although no friend of Zimmerman, wrote about him almost with grudging admiration:

> One bold operator organized a system which virtually made him ruler of the province for several years. In person or by agents he kept "open house," where the choicest brands of Champaign and cigars were free to all the peoples' representatives, from the town councilor to the cabinet minister; and it was the boast of one of these agents that when the speaker's bell rang for division, more members of the legislature were to be found in his apartments than in the library or any other single resort!

Not much is known about Zimmerman prior to his arrival in Canada in 1842. He was born the fifth son of a family of seven brothers and one sister on March 17, 1815, in Huntington, Pennsylvania. The family was of German extraction. He was orphaned at some stage and took charge of three younger brothers and sister. The impetus for his remarkable, albeit short, career may lie in having this responsibility thrust upon him. He left school at an early age and worked as a labourer. Although he is credited with having provided for the education of his siblings, little is now known of them. He appears to have been alone when he arrived in Canada with only a grey mare, a buggy, and a dollar or two (or so he frequently claimed). At some point his sister must have joined him, for he arranged her burial at St. David a short while before his own death. A brother, Martin, partnered his Niagara property development — but, curiously, was not listed as a director of the Zimmerman Bank, Samuel's other Niagara initiative, which he appeared to run for his sole benefit.

On his arrival in Canada, Zimmerman quickly found construction work on the Welland Canal and before long was bidding, with a partner James Oswald, for the job of rebuilding, in stone, several wooden locks in the region of Thorold. He and his partner were quickly recognized as effective organizers, tough masters who brooked no interruption of the work. His success brought a rising income and his natural acquisitive instincts led him, six years after his arrival, to begin making large land purchases on the Canadian side of Niagara Falls. Travels to England and the continent gave him a taste for fine living. His marriage in 1848 to Margaret Ann, daughter of wealthy Niagara-region businessman Richard Woodruff, perhaps gave him the incentive and improved means to acquire a residence truly reflective of his chosen lifestyle. The marriage, however, was short-lived. Margaret Ann died in 1851, after bearing two sons.

By 1853 Zimmerman owned much of the property in the vicinity of the Falls and pushed the incorporation of the town under the name Elgin, to honour then-governor general, Lord Elgin, who had established his residence nearby. A few years later the town was expanded and renamed Clifton. Later it became the modern city of Niagara Falls, Ontario.

There is no doubt that Zimmerman was the true father of Niagara Falls. In 1856 the *Welland Herald* claimed: "Perhaps no place in Canada has made such progress in so short a period of time, and I believe in few towns of the same population is there a greater circulation of ready money." The development of the town typified the Zimmerman approach. Everything was done on a grand scale. Water and gas works were constructed and streets laid out — then he began selling lots. Having purchased Clifton House, a local landmark hotel, Zimmerman proceeded to renovate it so that by the time he was finished the dining room could accommodate three hundred and the ballroom no less than one thousand. The *Herald* reporter was able to gasp with unrestrained local pride: "A year or two past, we had one grocery store, now about fourteen or fifteen, with upwards of twenty saloons and hotels, some of these equal to any kept in large cities."

Just how lavish the scale on which Zimmerman lived and entertained was can be judged by a celebrated dinner he gave in honour of his friend, the newly appointed governor of Barbados, Francis

Hincks. As inspector general of the Canadian union, it was Hincks who had shepherded the Municipal Loans Act through the legislature. By that act, municipalities were empowered to borrow from the province funds for subscribing to railways running through their districts. That opened up a vast pot of money, making many railway projects viable and offering generous pickings for influential and determined contractors. It was Hincks, too, as Canadian premier until his defeat in 1854, who had been the most influential member of the Board of Railway Commissioners that screened applications for charters. The dinner, given on October 31, 1855, at Clifton House, was one of the ways Zimmerman chose to express his appreciation to so dear a friend. Included in the three hundred-strong men-only dinner guest list were the then-premier, Sir Allan MacNab, and the man who, after Confederation, would become the country's first prime minister, John A. Macdonald.

The menu commenced with two soups, then the fish dishes and boiled meats — ham, mutton, and turkey — then roasts of ham, turkey, beef, and lamb. Also on offer were seven cold platters followed up by eleven entrees. For those who remained a trifle peckish, this was followed by venison, duck, and parry chicken served along with three styles of potato, onions, turnips, beets, and squash. Dessert featured plum pudding, rice pudding, apple pie, orange pie, quince tarts, wine jelly, lemon ice cream, grapes, walnuts, almonds, and raisins. It goes without saying that the very choicest vintages of wine were served. After appropriate toasts and speeches were made, the guests, joined by the women, trooped to the windows and grounds to witness the spectacular display of fireworks provided for their enjoyment. Then, around eleven o'clock, the ballroom doors were thrown open. One young gatecrasher who found his way into the galleries overlooking the dance floor wrote in his diary: "Such a splendor of dress I never saw before. Each one tried to outdo the other. There were very many pretty ladies there … I did not stay a great while for the splendor and brilliancy of the scene were bedizening." By 1:30 it was time for a late supper, then the party continued until about 4:00 a.m., when the pending departure of the early Toronto-bound train led many to leave.

In 1855 Zimmerman sold, en masse, the balance of the undeveloped property to a partnership that included Roswell Gardiner Benedict. Benedict, the same age as Zimmerman, arrived in Canada about five years later, after working as a civil engineer on railways in New York and Ohio. He met Zimmerman on the Welland Canal project. When Benedict was appointed as assistant to the chief engineer of the Great Western he successfully promoted the services of Zimmerman's firm as contractors for the eastern section of that route. Later, when Benedict took over the position of chief engineer for the railway he was able to certify Zimmerman's shoddy handiwork, approve dubious claims for cost overruns, and arrange early completion premiums on work completed well past deadlines. Zimmerman had much to be grateful to Benedict for. In light of that relationship, it cannot be ascertained whether the reported $200,000 Zimmerman was paid for the Niagara lots represented fair market value or not, but it was more than twenty times the amount he paid for it less than two years earlier. The new owners, however, continued to develop the city on a Zimmerman-like scale — deeding free land for the market square and various churches, laying down plank sidewalks, and planting shade trees.

Throughout these developments, Zimmerman was looking to his own comforts — on a scale that must have boggled his contemporaries. He took possession of a very substantial house on the escarpment facing the American Falls. This, however, was a mere *pied-à-terre*. He had something very much grander in mind — a fifty-two-acre preserve, fenced by iron railings and privet hedges. The development of his personal estate entailed the creation of extravagant formal gardens below the escarpment on the land where Niagara's Victoria Park is now situated. Gravel paths and drives were laid out and ornamental shrubbery was established. The whole was illuminated by gaslights fed by Zimmerman's newly constructed gasworks. There were fountains as well, the most noteworthy being that $15,000 extravagance that caught the attention of local citizens and survived his passing for so long. His stables were constructed at a cost of $18,000 and fine lodges built at each of the estate's four entrances. The house itself was never realized. Plans had been completed for an elegant mansion that was to cost $175,000. At the time of Zimmerman's death only the sandstone and brick foundations had been laid. A later owner built on these footings, but by all accounts the finished residence was a less imposing structure than Zimmerman had envisaged, and was long ago demolished.

His death dealt a blow to the building plans of St. Andrew's Church. Zimmerman, a Presbyterian, thought the congregation was being too conservative in their expansion plans and offered to personally pay the difference between those plans and the style of edifice he thought appropriate to the rapidly growing community. His offer was accepted, but his untimely death left the congregation without the promised funds and burdened for many years with a heavy debt.

Another Zimmerman enterprise was the proudly named Zimmerman Bank, established in 1854 under an 1850 act known as the Free Banking Act. Only six such institutions were ever founded. Under the act, the banks were limited to a single place of business and the banknotes were printed under the supervision of the government using plates supplied by the issuer. Every note was 100 percent backed by a deposit with the provincial treasury. For the bank, the sole advantage to this operation was the 6 percent return paid by the province on the reserved funds.

Changes in the legislation soon enabled the Zimmerman Bank to become a chartered institution, and with that came considerably greater leeway in the issuance of notes. The bank moved quickly to redeem the notes registered under the Free Banking Act for chartered notes. This allowed the bank to draw down its lendings to the treasury and put them to better use — and to benefit from "seigeniorage." That term refers to the fact that any holder of a banknote receives no interest, while the issuer is able to lend out the deposit. Rewarding as that perk may be, it was not for seigniorage that Zimmerman had set up his bank. It was to finance his business interests and his lifestyle. The bank served that purpose very well indeed, and the citizens of Niagara took pride in the further evidence of their community's importance that it represented.

Only after his death did some of the bank's more dubious operations come to light. At first, the Bank of Upper Canada (banker to the government) announced its readiness to redeem Zimmerman notes at face value. It was soon revealed, however, that while Zimmerman's estate held more than 98 percent of the authorized capital, less than half was paid up. Moreover, the Bank of Upper Canada had been involved in some shady dealings with the Zimmerman Bank — amongst other things, it had taken over responsibility for $247,960 worth of Zimmerman debt without

The Zimmerman Bank was founded in the 1850s and converted into one of the earliest chartered banks in 1856. The bank building, located on the corner of Bridge Street at Clifton Avenue (today Zimmerman Avenue) also served as post office and customs house. It was one of the more solid structures in Niagara Falls — even if the financial institution itself proved less poorly founded. After Zimmerman's death the true state of the bank's affairs were revealed and building itself became the Savoy Hotel — now long since demolished.

NIAGARA FALLS PUBLIC LIBRARY, D11311.

any collateral whatsoever. The instruction to that effect was boldly given to the government's banker by the receiver general of the province, the Honourable J.C. Morrison, member for Niagara and close personal friend of Zimmerman. Morrison had authorized direct government loans to Zimmerman without security and without even bothering to inform cabinet. At his death, the combined debt of Zimmerman and his bank to the Bank of Upper Canada exceeded half-a-million dollars. The bank's charter was sold to Chicago interests, and their pace of unauthorized note issuance quickly debauched the Zimmerman currency. The monumental, but uncompleted, Clifton estate fell into the hands of the Bank of Upper Canada, under whose authority Samuel Zimmerman's remains were exhumed and transported to nearby St. Davids.

Despite the importance of property development and banking to the Zimmerman wealth, he was known as a railway contractor and promoter. How did he parlay the brute skills of an uneducated labourer into a position of such influence and affluence? The answer is necessarily complex. He clearly relied partly on bluster. He was not a man to squirrel away a dollar earned, but could set it to work generating the illusion of greater wealth than he really enjoyed, or investing it sagely in cultivating friendships that would later pay staggering dividends. He undoubtedly made good money out of his rigorous management of the Welland Canal project, which would have constituted his seed capital. With the help of his engineering friend Benedict, he proceeded to milk the Great Western contract for much more than it was legitimately worth. In collusion with Benedict, Zimmerman added unnecessary miles to the right-of-way, built embankments to the absolute minimum standards and grades to their maximum permissible steepness, and in virtually every regard "scamped" the work. All of this was rewarded with full payment and generous bonuses.

However, only in the last few years of his short life was he able to leverage his ability to cutting corners with his ability to sway and, when necessary, to pervert. Then he was able to command the pervasive influence in railway matters that so incensed Thomas Keefer. The affair of the Cobourg and Peterborough Railway exemplifies the Zimmerman style close to its nadir.

Zimmerman was contracted to build the C&P, of which another of his professional cronies, Ira Spaulding (one of Benedict's partners in the Niagara development), was the civil engineer. As had been the case on the Great Western, the engineer approved alterations and improvements that constantly drove costs above the contract price. One outstanding feature of the line was the construction of a trestle bridge across a portion of Rice Lake. Three miles in length, one of

The earliest railway station at Clifton, the former name of Niagara Falls, pictured in 1859. The guests for Zimmerman's elaborate banquet in honour of his friend Francis Hinks would have arrived and departed from here, and so would many of those who attended Zimmerman's funeral.

NIAGARA FALLS PUBLIC LIBRARY, D11997.

the longest then in existence, the structure was opened in time for Christmas 1854. On New Year's Day ice movements shifted the southern portion of the trestle four feet off its base. Worse was to come with spring breakup. Over the ensuing six years the poorly designed and constructed bridge was closed for repairs more often than it was open, and was finally abandoned. Although the railway's board, comprised of neophyte local interests, protested the exorbitant overrun charges for Zimmerman's shoddy handiwork, validated by his engineering accomplice, they had no choice but to settle — Zimmerman simply refused to hand over the "finished" railway or the contractor's engines and rolling stock until they did!

The Great Western, having witnessed firsthand the Zimmerman technique, might have been expected to shy away from further collaboration with him. They made every effort to do so. When GWR interests proposed the Toronto and Hamilton Railway the British company directors sought to neutralize colonial competition by awarding the contract to the British firm of George Whythes. Zimmerman was not to be circumvented. Before legislative approval could be obtained, a tribute of £10,000 sterling was extracted, along with a commitment to contract him for the Sarnia extension.

By 1855 the Great Western was convinced that their single-track mainline was inadequate for the growing traffic. Apparently resigned to the inevitable, they enlisted the aid of the redoubtable Zimmerman. His price for ensuring passage of the necessary powers to double the track was the contract itself. By supreme irony the act shepherded through the legislature contained the following amending clause, to minimize delays to the GWR timetable:

> And Whereas it is doubtful that the sixth section of the statute passed in the sixteenth year of Her Majesty's Reign entitled, "An Act in addition to the general Railway Clauses Consolidation Act" was intended to apply to the Great Western Railway. And whereas the only draw-bridges on the line of

> the said Railway are situated as regards their proximity to stations and other circumstances that it is not considered necessary that the sixth section of the said Act should apply to the said Railway. Be it therefore enacted and declared that the said sixth section of the said last mentioned Act was not intended nor shall the same apply or be in force in regard to the said Great Western Railway, in so far as respects the bridge over the Desjardins Canal, nor to any swing bridge while the navigation is closed; anything in the said Act contained to the contrary notwithstanding.

The sixth section of the act of 1851 stipulated that all trains approaching a drawbridge must be brought to a halt and held for three minutes — failure to do so would result in a £100 fine. That provision was a direct consequence of the Norwalk, Connecticut, disaster several years earlier, when a passenger train plunged into an open draw causing forty-six deaths. While the Hamilton-bound train that tore apart the Desjardins Canal Bridge on March 12, 1857, was only travelling at a walking pace, had it been brought to a complete halt at the switch approaching the bridge the broken axle probably would have been obvious when the engine restarted, and the derailment on the bridge could have been completely avoided or greatly mitigated. What the convenient amendment contained in the Zimmerman-sponsored legislation accomplished was to allow the GWR to run their trains onto the bridge without stopping. That privilege very likely cost the act's champion, the irrepressible Zimmerman, his life — along with those of fifty-nine others.

The final chapter in the Zimmerman railway saga concerns the "Southern Railway." Although the Canada Southern Railway was eventually built, the very threat of its construction as a competitor to the Great Western was manipulated by Zimmerman in typically win-win style. Anxious to expand commercial development in the

Niagara region, Zimmerman had acquired two local interests: the Erie and Ontario Railway and the Niagara Harbour and Docks Company. The former one of the very earliest railways in Upper Canada had been originally built as a horse-powered portage route around the Falls. The latter was established on the Niagara River below Queenston (i.e., on the Lake Ontario side of the Falls). As early as 1853, Zimmerman was attempting to interest the Great Western in acquiring these assets. Had they done so, Zimmerman intended to lure a substantial amount of the Railway's heavy engineering away from Hamilton to the region of the Niagara Docks, once again to his huge personal advantage.

If the railway wouldn't bite, Zimmerman threatened to include the Erie and Ontario right-of-way as the initial section of a separate railway line that could be built south of the Great Western mainline and provide a substantially shorter route between Buffalo and Detroit than the GWR, while at the same time tapping a lot of the regional traffic the GWR was hoping to exploit.

He was able to convince the then-managing director of the Great Western, C.W. Brydges, that the company should purchase the Zimmerman assets, subject to board approval. The battle over this issue soured relationships between Brydges and MacNab, resulting in the latter's eventual dismissal from the board. In this instance, however, MacNab's view prevailed. MacNab was aware that Zimmerman had only recently purchased the dock company for £9,000 and was asking £179,000 for it. It seemed to MacNab that the exorbitant cost was not justified, largely because he believed that the purchases would not, as Zimmerman claimed, thwart eventual construction of a southern route by the Great Western. MacNab's view persuaded the board, Brydges agreement was countermanded, and Zimmerman's offer was refused.

Typically, Zimmerman then began to actively sponsor the threatened new independent southern route. Two projected railways were to be linked to form the major part of this route: the Woodstock and Lake Erie and Harbour Company and the Amherstburg and St.

Thomas Railway. By 1857 the contract for the former was already in Zimmerman's hands, and the board was packed with his associates. The latter railway posed something of a problem, as both Great Western and Zimmerman interests oversubscribed the capital. Claiming irregularities on the part of the Great Western interests, Zimmerman proceeded to hold a parallel organizational meeting in an Amherstburg hotel on August 7, 1856. At the very same hour the Great Western group were holding their meeting in the town hall! The result, for the time being, was two boards and two presidents.

By early 1857 things were going very much Zimmerman's way. In fact, the very meeting he left to take the ill-fated train had satisfactorily resolved many issues. Some reports said that the proposed charter of the southern route was actually found on his person when his body was recovered from the wreck.

Another report, that earlier that day he had removed a copy of his will from a deposit box at the Bank of Upper Canada and that it was found in his pocket, seems more credible. Less than four months earlier he had married for the second time. His second wife was Emmeline Dunn of Three Rivers, Quebec. If he had not already done so, it would have been a prudent time to review his estate.

Not much is known about his family after the accident. His estate was initially believed to be valued in the order of three million dollars — a very substantial sum for the times. In addition to his property holdings at Niagara, he owned large tracts of land in Hamilton and Toronto. He was the owner of a large side-wheeler steamboat that operated on Lake Ontario (named the *Zimmerman*) and leased another vessel, the *Peerless*. Even taking into account the many charges that undoubtedly could be levelled against his estate; the remaining fortune must have been immense. His wife almost immediately moved to Toronto with the two young sons of his previous marriage, John (age eight) and Richard (age six), who apparently frequently returned to visit their mother's family. Richard graduated in medicine from McGill University. Emmeline seems to have quickly severed her association with Samuel's memory, evident in the rather cavalier treatment his remains received — eventually interred without recognition beside his first wife. Emmeline remarried six years later, once again to an older man — a New York bachelor.

Many years later an aging relative of the Dunn family, living in Niagara, related yet another ironic twist in the convoluted fate that spared some and took the lives of others. (Zimmerman's second wife was a Dunn from Canada East, but the Dunn family was also highly influential in Canada West, so it may well be that it was through that local connection that he met her.) According to the tale related during the belated recognition of his gravesite in 1940, one of Zimmerman's last business enterprises was the purchase of timber rights north of Toronto, in Barrie. Apparently he had appointed Luther Dunn and his brother-in-law by his first marriage, James Woodruff, to supervise those operations. Zimmerman was in the process of winding up those operations and had visited the location prior to attending his business in Toronto. All three were initially going to return to Niagara together, but a last minute delay in closing the business caused Zimmerman to ask his associates to delay their immediate travel — assuring them that he would explain the delay to their families. Of course he was never able to fulfill that intention.

The short-term residence atop the escarpment was left empty until pressed into temporary use during a visit to Niagara by the Prince of Wales in 1860. After his brief stay the hurriedly assembled furnishings were again removed and the house was abandoned. A subsequent developer completed a less substantial mansion on the footings Zimmerman had intended for his own edifice. That house was subsequently demolished in the 1930s for no better reason than to avoid the taxes.

The story of Samuel Zimmerman is intriguing both for what it reveals about mid-nineteenth-century business practices as well as for what has now largely been lost to posterity. Since Zimmerman was not quite forty-two when he died, and since his skills at financial machination had been honed in such a short time, it is fascinating to contemplate what role in the affairs of Canada he might have played had he not perished in the freezing waters of the Desjardins Canal. Canadian Confederation occurred only ten years later and it was only the promise of a transcontinental railway that made the agreement to unite possible. Could Samuel Zimmerman have held himself aloof from so seductive a "honey pot" as the Canadian Pacific Railway? The "Road Van Horne Built" could have become "Samuel's Swansong." Might he have been tempted away from his aversion to political service? Could Zimmerman have been Canada's first post-Confederation prime minister? The answer to those questions became entirely academic a few seconds after a locomotive with a fractured axle ran, without stopping, onto a wooden bridge over the Desjardins Canal.

CHAPTER FIVE

A Cast of Players

Few, if any, inventions have had as dramatic an impact on so broad a segment of society as the introduction of train travel in the mid-1800s. Less than half a decade before the Desjardins accident there were limited options for travelling the relatively short distance between Toronto and Hamilton. One could travel the laborious, uncomfortable route by road or by the more comfortable and predictable passage on a lake steamer. More often than not, unless you were of a certain class, you simply did not make the trip at all. Looking back from a modern vantage point, what is truly outstanding is how egalitarian train travel was in that era. On the same train and destined to meet the same fate were Timothy Doyle, about whom nothing is now known other than that he was a young shoemaker, and, at the opposite end of the social scale, Samuel Zimmerman, the rich and influential capitalist. Only a few years earlier Doyle would doubtless not have contemplated taking his family on such a journey. Zimmerman, on the other hand, must have delighted in his ability to hammer out lucrative new deals with alacrity and comfort. For each, train travel opened new opportunities. It was the great equalizer.

If train travel was generally egalitarian, the 4:10 GWR train to Hamilton on March 12, 1857, nevertheless carried a noteworthy collection of the most wealthy and influential Canadians — along with not a few of the region's more interesting "characters." Peering back through the past 150 years, one often feels left with only a two-dimensional image of the participants in the tragedy. Capsule biographies, even if written in comparatively recent times, frequently tend to regurgitate the same superficial anecdotes from when the subjects were still alive. Scarcely any biography of Zimmerman fails to mention his claim to have arrived in the country with only a grey horse and a buggy. An even better example of the biographical genre is provided by the yarn spun about Captain James Sutherland. An obituary in the *Hamilton Spectator* first noted that Sutherland received a silver service from an appreciative English stockholder in 1847. The inscription is duly and superfluously spelled out. This nugget is repeated in many biographical synopses of Sutherland. That it in no way illuminates the character of the man, matters not. While so much of who he was and what he accomplished has been obscured by time, that useless fragment remains with us. Yet all is not lost. Simply by understanding better the history of the era — its politics and its business and social practices — one can piece together vignettes that capture the essence of some of those involved.

Take Thomas Clark Street, for example. The press of the era was quick to highlight his escape with just a fractured collarbone and an injury to his right arm. The municipal council of the County of Welland, however, passed a memorable resolution, the first part of which somewhat cursorily mourned the death of Zimmerman and John Morley, the Thorold plough-maker, then goes on to address the status of the survivor, Thomas Clark Street, Esquire, of Clark Hill, "Whose intelligence and widely-known abilities as a business man, and whose elevated social position have secured to him universal regard and provincial fame, but whose valuable life was by the merciful providence of God spared on the occasion before mentioned." Who was this man whose salvation inspired such effusion?

Many news reports at the time characterized Samuel Zimmerman as "if not the wealthiest, then one of the two wealthiest." Street was that other man. As fate would have it they travelled on the same train. Street rode in the first car from which few survived, and lived. Zimmerman rode the second car, in which most lived, but he died. Since we know how ephemeral Zimmerman's wealth proved to be, we can deduce that Street was indeed the province's richest resident. When he eventually died, in 1872, his estate was valued somewhere between three and four million dollars.

Street was a patrician, born into a wealthy Connecticut loyalist family. Starting in 1844, he parlayed a major inheritance into a broad-based business empire that saw him become president of the Niagara Falls Suspension Bridge Company and the Gore Bank, as well as a director of other banks and of the British American Assurance Company. He was sufficiently involved in shipping to have been lumped together with Captain Sutherland and Samuel Zimmerman as "the other prominent ship-owner involved in the disaster." He likely would not have relished being so characterized. He would have known Zimmerman very well — they were both big frogs in the same pond — yet it is hard to imagine them having much in common. They indeed belonged in different cars on the ill-fated train.

Street, in his early forties at the time of the accident, had already served as a Conservative member in the legislature. He was first elected in 1851, defeated in 1854, and then re-elected in 1861. He later served in John A. Macdonald's first post-Confederation cabinet. While Zimmerman was still occupied in the construction of his mansion, Street's magnificent house, Clark Hill, which overlooked the rapids above Niagara Falls, was recognized as the most opulent in the district. The estate's magnificence was further enhanced by his purchase of the islands below the house and their conversion into a private park.

Some have claimed that Street's involvement in politics was meant to further his business interests. That was scarcely grounds for censure in the mid-1800s. The demands emerging in a developing

Thomas Clark Street's reputation as being Canada's richest citizen proved to be better founded than his fellow Clifton (Niagara) resident, Zimmerman. Both were aboard the death train. Street, however, survived — one of the few travelling in the train's first car to do so. He sustained only minor injuries.

NIAGARA FALLS PUBLIC LIBRARY, D10558.

economy conformed happily to the resources and rewards commanded by a capitalist elite. As an autocratic politician who was content to use his "landed" position as a mortgage holder to "persuade" voters to support him, he took a surprisingly reformist view favouring representation by population. According to one biographer, this was not so much a reflection of his faith in the common man as it was a very practical appreciation of the consequences of it being withheld.

Although Street was obviously very much a participant in the Desjardins Canal disaster, he seems to have been strangely untouched by it. He suffered no serious injury, despite being in the most devastated car. He was either deliberately aloof and uncommunicative (as might be fitting to his "station") or else genuinely bewildered by the event. To reporters he could/would not provide an account of the accident and claimed to know nothing that happened before being extricated from the ruins.

One victim who would undoubtedly have been less reticent in describing his experiences was the Reverend Alfred Booker. But fifty-seven-year-old Booker, travelling in the first car, had no opportunity to express his feelings — he perished in the wreck. Like any preacher, Booker made his living out of speaking. In fact, he had only boarded the train at Wellington (now a part of Burlington, Ontario) just a couple of stops before the bridge, shortly after delivering what had become a weekly afternoon sermon in the town hall.

Although such outreach activities were undoubtedly part of the function of his office, Booker probably would have resented being characterized as a "preacher." He more likely perceived his role as that of elder or pastor. A determinedly autocratic individual, he seemed much more concerned with maintaining doctrinal discipline within his flock than with expanding the church membership. One can almost hear him uttering the old aphorism that there are two ways of looking at things — your way and God's way (with, of course, the implicit assumption that Booker's way aligned with the latter).

Once again, one must be careful to evaluate people in the context of their era. The autocratic intolerance of Alfred Booker appears preposterous in the modern era of ecumenism. In the 1850s the churches were routinely full and there were relatively few who dared to exclude themselves from at least professing religious belief. To the professional clergyman, the challenge was less that of acquiring new Christian converts than a matter of developing "brand loyalty." A multitude of schisms and subdivisions characterized most denominations at the time. Even in the context of the era, however, Booker appears to have been a notably rigid and petty authoritarian.

No one can question his commitment — forged out of the doubts of youthful sincerity. As a seventeen-year-old in Nottingham, England, he met up with a friend whose father had ordered him to attend the evening chapel service (as proof of his unwilling attendance, Booker's friend was under instructions to return home with the "text" — i.e., the Scriptural quotation on which the sermon was based). To keep his friend company, Booker attended the service. So moved was he by the sermon that he commenced a lifetime dedication to bible study that set him on the road to his calling. At thirty he became the pastor at Park Street Church in Nottingham.

When he was forty-two years old, with most, if not all, of his eight children already born he felt the missionary call. Although unlettered, Booker had developed a proficiency in French and hence it was to Canada East that the family first sailed in 1842. For reasons now obscure, he abandoned his ambitions in Quebec and fixed his attentions on Hamilton. In a remarkable exercise in faith and conviction he addressed a letter to the "Baptists of Hamilton," enjoining them to hold prayer meetings until he arrived to take over their pastoral instruction. Not knowing where to deliver the letter, the Hamilton postmaster handed it to Philo Dayfoot, who ran a shoe store opposite the post office. Under Dayfoot's guidance a small group of Baptists formed and eventually welcomed Booker and his family in the spring of 1843. The congregation's first services were held in the police station and then, later, a local schoolhouse. What was to become Park Street Baptist Church was officially founded in January 1844 and that same month held its first baptismal service.

That first baptism was held at a local stream. Church records show that in order to conduct the ritual for the four candidates "The ice had to be cut to allow the baptism. There was a large congregation present and many that never saw the ordinance administered in its primitive form before." Primitive it certainly was! One has to admire not only the pluck of the celebrants, but also the zeal of Alfred Booker, forty-four years old, standing in the frigid water long enough to ensure the complete immersion of each candidate.

And complete immersion it had to be! What set Booker's Baptists aside from other congregations that would spring-up in the region was that they were "regular." Not only did this mean that church membership was closed to those who had not undergone baptism by complete immersion, it meant that members of non-approved churches, even other Baptists, could not share communion with the Park Street congregation. Even bible studies, notionally open to "others who wished to attend," followed a carefully prescribed pattern. Tea and plain bread and butter were served (definitely no cakes). Sitting at the head, Booker worked around the table soliciting suggested passages of Scripture and then personally expounding on their meaning. Even the participation of others was tightly regulated. To join in you had either to be a member of the Park Street church or be introduced by a member, having first received the approval of the deacons or pastor.

This sort of doctrinal and disciplinary rigidity was undoubtedly practised in other churches of that period, but reading the assortment of charges and countercharges that form part of the history of Booker's administration, one cannot help but get the sense of a man clinging to "principle" and "authority" with a tenacity bordering on paranoia. In one instance, in which he easily defended himself against a charge the he was too exclusive, he refused the complainant the right to resign from the church. Instead, Booker oversaw his expulsion.

Such a procedure might appear nothing more than a petty trifle today, but at that time, without an appropriate "letter" attesting to the character of its holder, one could easily be blackballed by other congregations. Acrimony surrounded the wording and issuance of such letters. The Park Street congregation argued on biblical grounds that: "They went out from us, but they were not of us; for if they had been of us, they would have continued with us." (1st John, Chapter 2, verse 19.) Such Orwellian reasoning prevented the discreet withdrawal of those who came into conflict with Booker's dictatorial stance. Dissidents from the Park Street church formed the John Street church, but the former refused to recognize the latter as being of "the same faith and order." When one couple refused to accept any "letter" unless addressed to the John Street group, they were expelled for "insubordination." During the years 1850–51, Park Street lost, through desertion and expulsion, some forty members, twenty-seven of whom eventually settled in the John Street congregation.

Of the high-profile victims of the Desjardins accident, Booker is definitely one of the "characters." Something of a parody of Victorian clergymen, he nevertheless comes across as being intensely human, even if the aspects he exhibited are not especially elevating. Someone with such a strong personality must have had an intimidating impact on his family. Whether cowed by his dominance or compelled by the intensity of his conviction, several of his immediate family formed part of the inaugural congregation. Over the years, about thirty Bookers have been active on the church role and one of his sons, William, was a charter member and served for almost fifty years with the church. The family was not without political and social influence either. At one point, a portion of Booker's income came from land granted to the church by Allan MacNab. One of Booker's grandsons briefly served as Hamilton's mayor.

The greatest irony in the relationship between the Bookers and the Great Western Railway is not that the railway took the good reverend's life — after all, that was just an accident of fate. What is perhaps most intriguing, is Booker's son Alfred Booker Junior's tangential involvement with the GWR and the wreck. Due to the last-minute illness of the intended marshall of the parade that welcomed the inaugural Great Western train into Hamilton in 1854, the ceremonial duty fell to Alfred Junior. At the head of his artillery company he triumphantly welcomed the inception of a service that would claim his father a few years later. Of course, the same Alfred Junior rushed his militia to the scene of the disaster to mount guard on the accumulating corpses in the station sheds, among which was that of his father.

Easy as it is to be mildly repelled by the rather antagonistic image projected by the humourless Booker, it is easier to be attracted to the picture of fun-loving affability that Adam Ferrie casts through the years of history. Ferrie was only twenty-four years old when he died.

The Ferrie family had an illustrious history, descended from Admiral Ferrier, the grandee of Spain, who led the Spanish Armada in the 1500s. That invasion of Britain proving abortive, the discreet Ferrier chose to settle in Ayrshire, Scotland, rather than face the uncertain welcome of a conquered hero in Spain. In 1777 Adam Ferrie was born (grandfather of the young victim at Desjardins). Adam Senior (later the Honourable Adam Ferrie) became adept in the textile trade and branched out into hardware and grocery wholesaling in Britain and the Continent. Between 1815 and 1820 he lost most of his commercial fortune due to imprudently guaranteeing the debt of business associates. To recoup his losses, Ferrie expanded his horizons to include trade with the West Indies, where he lived in Jamaica for several years, and to Brazil. In 1824 he formed a partnership with a Montrealer, with a view to opening up the Canadian trade. After Ferrie's partner proved unreliable Ferrie himself visited Canada, eventually establishing a business and financial enterprise in Montreal.

His sons Colin and Adam (a common family name — this one being the uncle of the train victim) were the ones who expanded the family business into Southern Ontario. In Doon (in the region of present-day Kitchener) Adam oversaw the creation of a sophisticated integrated enterprise comprised of a gristmill, sawmill, distillery, tavern, granary, and cooperage along with housing. The whole complex was supplied by an impressively constructed dam — the sturdiness of which proved illusory. In 1840 it collapsed, precipitating Adam's humiliating replacement as manager by his brother Robert. Adam's choice of wife had been vehemently opposed by his father. His business failure and the generally deteriorating financial climate exacerbated family frictions, and by the time of his death, only a few years later, Adam was heavily in debt to his family and a broken man.

Colin, father of the unfortunate railway victim, although by any measure successful, appears to have been cut from different cloth than his own father. A contemporary account styles him as being "of medium height, fair complexion, and very pleasant manners." He represented Hamilton in the Legislative Assembly of Upper Canada from 1836–41 His election as Hamilton's first mayor in 1847 was not by general plebiscite, but by a vote of his fellow aldermen. His brief term

These two images capture the impact of the tragedy. The photograph of Adam Ferrie was most likely taken around the time of his marriage, July 2, 1856. From a prominent family, with all the right connections and a newly acquired legal practice, Ferrie was a young man apparently slated for success until he boarded the ill-fated train. His bride, the former Mary Woodley Dallas (pictured here some fifteen years later), was an exotic young seventeen-year-old. Ferrie could not have known when he died that Mary was already four weeks pregnant with his son.

ADAM FERRIE: HAMILTON PUBLIC LIBRARY, LOCAL HISTORY & ARCHIVES.
MARY WOODLEY DALLAS: COURTESY OF MARY HAWKINS/TOM STEWART.

came under considerable criticism after he equivocated on the issue of acquiring parkland, to the discomfort of his peers. He resigned when deteriorating economic circumstances threatened his private interests and raised questions about the propriety of his rising indebtedness to the Gore Bank, of which he was the founder and in which the family were major shareholders. He died in 1856 and, in part, his obituary in the *Hamilton Spectator* ran: "Although a prominent citizen, Mr. Ferrie was of a retiring disposition, and seldom took any public part, except by the urgent request of his fellow townsmen."

Whatever he may have lacked in terms of driving ambition he certainly made up for in terms of wealth and creature comforts. Upon his marriage he acquired land from Allan MacNab upon which to build the family home. While some reports suggest the residence was a wedding gift, his father disavowed that claim. In 1836 the building cost something between six and seven thousand pounds. While York Street was dominated by Dundurn Castle, the palatial home of Allan MacNab, next in terms of opulence was the Ferrie house: West Lawn.

The younger Adam Ferrie would have been just four years old when the family moved into West Lawn. What a childhood it would have been. The solid two-storey grey mansion commanded an uninterrupted view of the bay, and the grounds were opulently landscaped with lawns and flowerbeds. At the road there was a keeper's lodge and ornate iron gate through which a circular drive ran to the front entrance on the south face. On the east, French windows reached floor to ceiling and when natural light was insufficient chandeliers were suspended from decorative ceiling pieces. Each room had its own fireplace. Some, like the upstairs library, had two. The floors were laid with pine and in the centre stood a broad, curving walnut staircase. On the north and east sides behind that staircase was a single spacious room, eminently suitable for elegant entertaining.

West Lawn was not the only luxury young Adam would have known. He was a frequent and welcome visitor at his Uncle Adam's property in Doon. There he enjoyed all the comforts and pleasures of a country estate.

As Adam grew older he was boarded at the Toronto Academy. But life there was not without its problems. In one letter, now held by the Hamilton library, he wrote to his Uncle Robert about some startling events in the school. In an unnecessarily detailed and slightly pompous letter, which reflected his mere fourteen years of age, he detailed the discovery of the audacious criminal activities of a schoolmate. With a mature writing hand he detailed the value of goods taken from each student and waxed somewhat sanctimonious in observing: "What shall it profit a man if he gain the whole world and lose his soul at the last?" Still, one has to wonder at the impertinence of the confessed thief whom Adam claimed: "In a Latin Dictionary that he had stolen from John Cook he had written: 'From my aged and esteemed friend W. McNaughten, the cause of my coming to Toronto to study for the ministry.'" One wonders, in light of future developments and the extreme detail of his account, whether or not Adam himself may have been considered a possible suspect in the series of thefts.

The circumstances are no longer known, but a year later (in 1848) Adam was expelled from the academy. His Uncle Robert, writing to his sister Rachel, sounded quite irate at the behaviour of the school's principal. "You will have heard of Master Adam having been turned away from the Toronto Academy. I think under the circumstances that Mr. Gale might have written to Colin to take Adam away from the Academy, and not have sent him home."

Uncle Robert clearly had something of a soft spot for his nephew. You can almost see the twinkle in his eye when he writes to his own father (the Honourable Adam) after one of his visits to Doon in 1850: "Adam is turning out a fine young man and has improved much of late. He is quite a talker. A young lady told me that he said he has sown his wild oats and had given up sinning and drinking. That speech amused me very much." Doon was clearly something of a refuge for the young Adam. In that same letter his uncle indicates that Adam had been looking forward to an impending visit with a party of friends, which would include Sir Allan MacNab's daughter.

Whatever wild oats the privileged Adam Ferrie might have sown, by the time of his death he was beginning to assert the promise that his background had prepared him for. Only the previous year he had redeemed his academic record by graduating from Trinity College, been called to the bar, and appointed notary public. After briefly articling with the legal firm of Burns and Duggan he had opened up his own practice in Hamilton and, according to the Kingston *British Whig*, had "in a very short time acquired a business which showed the confidence placed in his capacity and integrity."

As further evidence of settling down, just eight months before his death on July 2, 1855, he was married to Mary Woodley Dallas by Reverend J.G. Geddis, dean of Hamilton's Christ Church Cathedral. The ceremony was a large and elaborate affair. Seventeen-year-old Mary was a fitting bride, and her background, as so often emerges when examining the characters of the time, confirms that mid-nineteenth-century Canada was vastly different from the backwoods farming stereotype so often portrayed. People, at least the affluent, were internationally mobile.

Mary was christened August 8, 1838, in Christ Church, Barbados, daughter of Dr. John Isaac and Eliza Dallas. Her grandfather Charles seems to have been a sugar plantation owner. Around 1850, when she was about twelve years old, the family left Barbados. After a brief stay in Tobago they appeared in Hamilton. Even to the worldly Adam, Mary must have seemed an exotic creature.

Despite their substantial wealth and undoubted influence, tragedy seemed to dog the Ferries. It might not be going too far to draw some modest parallels with the Kennedy clan of modern America. The Ferrie family was large and spread across the region. Adam's death at Desjardins made him the nineth member to have died in a twelve-month period. As early news of the disaster trickled into the Legislature, it was even rumoured that Adam's brother, then a member of the house, had perished along with him.

Perhaps saddest of all, on that cold March day when he met his fate Adam likely did not know that his bride was four weeks pregnant. On November 5, 1857, young Adam (yet another namesake) was born in the home of his grandmother — herself a widow of barely a year. He lived just two years, three months, and sixteen days. Father and son are both buried in the same plot in Hamilton Cemetery. Their marker, a deliberately broken column signifying premature death, seems entirely fitting.

Records reveal that several months after she was widowed a court action was undertaken against the Great Western on Mary's behalf, attempting to prove liability and recover damages. Efforts by the railway to "discover" her financial position hint that she was by no means destitute after Adam's death. Unfortunately, the outcome of the case has been obscured by history.

Mary's grief must have been intense, but scarcely eight months after the death of her son she appeared in St. Michael Parish, Barbados, where she was married for the second time to a man by the name of Charles Tinling, postmaster of Barbados and twenty-two years her senior. She gave birth to two daughters who died aged eight and three years old. After Charles's death in 1875, Mary returned to Hamilton and died in 1882.

The accomplishments of several of the victims conflict with any simplistic image we might have of late-colonial Canada. As long as 150 years ago, the country had clearly progressed beyond being a simple resource economy. John Morley was thirty-five years old and the father of four when he died in the wreck. To say that the Thorold resident was a plough maker easily conveys the wrong message. This was no simple blacksmith hammering out crude instruments. The plough Morley created was an invention — a crafted design that had gained wide recognition for its effectiveness. More importantly, Morley's plough was a mass-produced product. He had commissioned some $10,000 or $12,000 worth of the pattern to be manufactured that spring. The reason for his journey on the ill-fated train was as part of a sales trip to drum up agents in Hamilton and Toronto to market his product. Morley's entrepreneurial expansion would not have been possible had it not been for the spread of the railways. Ploughs are heavy and cumbersome. Delivery across a broad inland region would not have been practical. Of course, the marketing trip that killed him would not have been as easily contemplated either.

The funeral of passenger Ralph Wade in Cobourg, Ontario, might conjure up a more conventional image of nineteenth-century rural Canada. Picture a country homestead in late winter, and a large crowd of farmers gathering to help mourn the death of one of their fellows. As the assembly begins to swell, merchants and mechanics and professionals can be seen among their numbers, forming-up into a procession one hundred carriages long to carry Ralph Wade to the burial ground by St. Peter's Church.

Even the face of agriculture was changing. Wade's obituary refers to him as an agriculturist, a label that suggests an analytical and scientific approach to farming. In a world just a few decades from rough tree clearing and root grubbing, men like Ralph Wade were transforming the business of farming. Wade imported large numbers of cattle and sheep to improve his herds. He entered and won prizes at local and national fairs and even, at a time when many were only beginning to move about within the vicinities of their birth, had managed to win several prizes for his grain at the Paris World's Fair.

While scientific methods were on the ascendancy, the story of John Henderson underscores a reality that still rings true today — it is hard to earn a decent living from pure science alone. Henderson, born in Leicestershire, England, was known as a professional "telegraphic engineer." That label must have been much more impressive then than it is today. A man who understood the mysteries of communication through wires, and could construct the necessary contraptions to do so, would doubtless have been seen as a very clever person. Henderson, however, clearly possessed even more scientific skills. He had been principal assistant to Professor Airey of Greenwich Observatory, and had, in fact, been offered the position of head of the observatory in Australia by the good professor. He turned that opportunity down to take the position of chief clerk of the mechanical department of the Great Western Railway. He must have intended that as a mere stepping stone toward more lucrative employment in Canada. He held that job for only about two years before becoming the Canadian agent for the Cyclops Iron Works. Manufacturing and marketing were where the money was to be made in Canada. How did Henderson start his Canadian experience as a rather mundane employee of a railway? That's simple. His brother-in-law was none other than C.J. Brydges, the managing director of the Great Western Railway.

Thomas Benson, of Port Hope, was another prominent victim. He had emigrated with his parents from his birthplace, Fintona, Ireland, when he was fifteen years old. The family originally settled in New York State, but within three years had established itself in Kingston, Ontario, where Thomas was educated. Out of respect for his family's nebulous objections, he gave up his legal ambitions and embarked instead on a rather ill defined "mercantile life." Whatever that entailed, he must have been accomplished at it, since his reputation as a trader grew — first at Kingston, where he married Alicia Maria Lowe in 1827, and subsequently in Port Hope, where he moved in 1832. During the rebellion of 1837 he served as captain of a company of volunteers, assigned to duties at Chippewa and Navy Island. When disturbances broke out again in 1839, he was commissioned as captain and paymaster in the 3rd Battalion of Incorporated Militia, and was stationed at Niagara until it was disbanded in 1845.

He then established himself as a successful miller in Peterborough, served as that town's first mayor, and subsequently sat on council. He was seen as a devout member of the Church of England, and avid supporter of the Upper Canada Bible Society. One contemporary observer noted that "being a ready, fluent, and eloquent speaker, with a well-stored mind, he occupied a foremost place on every platform where the claims of Christianity, philanthropy, or public enterprise, were put forth." That same person regretted that Benson, a political liberal-conservative, eschewed the opportunity to run for the provincial legislature.

That reluctance may have stemmed from some political unpleasantness during his period in Peterborough, which may have driven him to relocate to Port Hope, about twenty-five miles away in 1853. In 1850 Mayor Benson and his council awarded the contract for the new Peterborough Town Hall and Market House to a Toronto architect, rather than favour a local architect who had already earned some acclaim for his design of public buildings in the region. Feelings could apparently run very deep in colonial Canada, the Peterborough newspaper overlooked his contribution in reporting on the building's ceremonial opening and pointedly failed even to publish his obituary.

The obituary in the *Port Hope Tri-Weekly Guide*, however, was fulsome in its praise for its adopted citizen. Noting in part:

> Mr. Benson was one of the most public spirited and prominent citizens of Port Hope. His death has created a void in our midst, which will not be readily filled. The *Globe* and other Toronto papers in giving the list of killed by the late fearful accident, speak of Mr. Benson as a merchant of Port Hope — we would correct the error into which our contemporaries have fallen. Many years ago he was in the mercantile business in this town, but at the time of his death he was Secretary and Treasurer of the Port Hope, Lindsay, and Beaverton Railway. He assumed that post at the formation of the Company, and by his eminent business capacity conducted the corporation through more than one financial crisis. The loss of such a Secretary and Treasurer, at this particular juncture will be deeply felt by the Railway board and the town.

END OF THE LINE

At the time many railway schemes were devised to link communities along the northern shores of Lake Ontario with the projected route of the Grand Trunk Railway between Montreal, Toronto, and points west. Originally chartered in 1846 as the Peterborough and Port Hope Railway, the Port Hope, Lindsay & Beaverton Railway, of which Benson was named secretary and treasurer, was in direct competition with the Cobourg and Peterborough Railway fiasco constructed by the Zimmerman-Spaulding team that suffered the ignominious fate of seeing its newly constructed bridge sink into Rice Lake. The charter was renewed as the Port Hope, Lindsay & Beaverton Railway around the time of Benson's appointment and the first trains were running within a few months of his death. Eventually the railway was renamed yet again, as the Midland Railway, and formed a strategic link between Port Hope on Lake Ontario and Midland on Lake Huron. It appears that when he met his death on the Desjardins Canal Bridge, Thomas Benson was actually travelling in his official railway capacity.

Clearly Benson's esteem in the town rested on far more than his position with the railway. The commercial and civic interests of himself and his twelve children (some of whom became prominent in the legal circle from which Thomas was excluded) elevated the Benson name to high regard, as evidenced that before and during his funeral, every shop in town closed its doors and it was reported that the sidewalks along the route of his cortège were thronged with residents of the town and area.

Every death in the disaster was lamentable. Some, however, were more poignant than others. Who could not be moved by the calamity that befell the Doyle family with father, mother, and young son killed along with one of the father's brothers and the two young orphans with their surviving uncle left shivering and shocked on the edge of the broken ice? Others were orphaned at the canal. Thirty-five-year-old John Russell and his thirty-year-old wife, Ann, perished — leaving behind five children, the oldest of whom was just nine years old. John was a railway contractor and the family had apparently undergone some financial difficulties, which appeared to have been resolved. Ann had just returned from Europe (presumably England, where she was born). Whether or not this trip was related to the shift in their fortunes or a celebration of their return to solvency is not known. What is known is that John had travelled to Toronto to meet her and escort her the last few miles home to Brantford, close to Hamilton.

Their obituary was published in the *Christian Messenger* and the prose reflects both the Victorian love of hyperbole and the expected concerns of that journal. The few paragraphs contain very few temporal particulars about the couple, but an abundance of detail concerning their spiritual condition. John, apparently after years of moral living but wavering commitment, had only shortly before "seen the light" and experienced a religious conversion. "A few more fleeting months spent in trifling with the affairs of salvation" trumpeted the *Christian Messenger*, "and what would have been his fate and doom when he was precipitated into the chasm of death in a moment, and his soul called into eternity in such an awful sudden manner?" The family seems to have experienced some financial difficulty that they had surmounted. Of Ann, the *Messenger* piously uttered: "Years had rolled away, her husband had been brought to a saving knowledge of the truth, the sun of temporal prosperity had clearly begun to shine on every earthly concern, when lo! with the celerity of a passing moment she was called to meet death in the cold waters of the fatal canal, leaving children, and all earthly things for ever behind her."

Another family that death seemed to be whimsically stalking that March was the Browns. Thirty-two-year-old Charles Brown of Galt, Ontario, accompanied by his brother, had travelled to Toronto to attend the funeral of his father. With the elder Brown's remains conveyed to the Necropolis early that afternoon, Charles's duties were concluded and he returned to a friend's house, preparing to return home to Galt. His friend urged him to stay over, but Charles was anxious to rejoin his sisters who had remained in Galt, and so insisted on taking the 4:10 that very afternoon.

Observing how society was adapting to the rapid pace of progress makes an interesting aside. On one hand, there is the extended Doyle family — brothers and children — jaunting across southern Ontario for some unknown purpose. On the other, the apparent reluctance of the Galt sisters to accompany their brother on the relatively short trip to Toronto, even for their father's funeral. For his solicitous concern over his sister's well-being, Charles ended up occupying the same vault as his father just four days after the latter's funeral. His brother, apparently less concerned about his sisters' situation, accepted the friend's offer, stayed over, and lived. Even then, the sister's anxieties were not over — for a time it was believed that both brothers had travelled together and might have both perished.

The obituary penned by the Reverend John Butler for the Reverend Dr. Heise perhaps tells us less about the latter clergyman and more of the detachment of the local establishment from the foreigner. Butler wrote:

> Of his former history I am almost entirely ignorant. He told me that he emigrated from Germany, about eight or nine years since, to the United States, where he remained until 1854. He was introduced to me as a teacher of German which language I studied with him for some time…. He had been, I understood, a preacher among the Lutherans, in Philadelphia, and at some other places in the United States.

In a classically backhanded manner the Reverend Butler praises his dead colleague.

> He was a man of good abilities, especially for language, and who had not neglected the improvement of his intellect. His manner was unpretending, simple and humble ... and on the whole was one who tried, in my opinion, to do his duty to God and to his fellow-men.

The astonishing lack of familiarity with his life displayed by Dr. Heise's eulogist might be forgiven if the task had been assigned him as a courtesy for a departed professional colleague. Yet, not only had Butler studied German with Heise he had shared his roof with him: "Shortly after I knew him, he asked to come and board in my house. His request was complied with, and he remained a member of my family until he was so suddenly removed." If Heise was treated as a member of Butler's family, one can only speculate on what that family found to chat about in their leisure hours!

What we can deduce of Heise's life was that he was an earnest and studious young man who was anxious to follow his calling. The bishop of Toronto had ordained him as a deacon and he was expected soon to be elevated to the priesthood.

We know rather more of Captain James Sutherland — even beyond the fact that he was the recipient of an inscribed silver service. Sutherland was a veritable "sea dog" of the old school, bluff and self-willed. His life reads something like a history of the marine era when sail was giving way to steam on the seas and railways were eroding the supremacy of inland water transport.

Sutherland left his birthplace in the Orkney Islands when he was seventeen to serve under sail. In the employ of the Hudson's Bay Company he sailed with Sir John Franklin into Hudson Bay. He sailed the Baltic and south Atlantic, and was once stranded for sixteen hours with a broken collarbone off the coast of Prussia. He was mate of the *Royal William*, the first steamship to cross the Atlantic, and captained the *Europe*, which was the first transatlantic steamer to land at Quebec, and later the *Unicorn*.

END OF THE LINE

In 1831, while still only twenty-six years old, Sutherland settled in Canada and took up a succession of Great Lakes steamship commands. By 1840 he was captain of a new, fast vessel, the *Niagara*. When the owners sold that ship and he was given charge of the slower *St. George*, he was apparently quite chagrined. On one occasion his old command was seen astern of, and gaining on, the *St. George*. Sutherland supposedly grimaced, hitched up his trousers, and muttered: "So she is after us is she? Well we will soon pay her off in her own kind and be after her shortly."

His driving ambition was to not merely to captain steamships, but to be an owner. That goal was realized and in 1846 the *Magnet* was launched. The vessel had been designed and fabricated on the Scottish Clyde and shipped over to be assembled at the Niagara Docks. The British government subscribed a large portion of the stock on the proviso that her design would accommodate rapid conversion to a naval vessel in the event of another war with the United States.

As a proprietor, rather than just a captain, Sutherland's fortune began to change dramatically. So profitable was the *Magnet* that he was able to invest the surplus cash in extensive lumber and lands acquisitions, two sure bets for nineteenth century investors. When

Captain James Sutherland was a respected mariner, who was fated to die in just a few feet of frigid water. Sutherland cherished his command of his steamship, the **Magnet***.*

HAMILTON MUSEUM OF STEAM AND TECHNOLOGY, CITY OF HAMILTON.

he died at the age of fifty-two he was able to boast of considerable wealth and even greater influence. The *Kingston British Whig* (Kingston having been a frequent call of the captain) asserted that: "Next to Mr. Zimmerman, Captain Sutherland was better known than any of his fellow sufferers."

The *Hamilton Spectator* lauded Sutherland as:

> Frank, generous, manly, open-hearted, always ready to sympathize with the unfortunate and relieve the distressed, he was a fine sample of a British sailor, to which profession he was bred, having been almost cradled on the stormy seas which surround the home of his youth in the Northern part of his native land. The loss of such a man is itself a public calamity, for it leaves a gap in the social fabric which is not easily filled up.

Seafaring was still a noble tradition at the time — for some families the only calling. Sutherland had been born into such a tradition. He was the nephew of James Sutherland of the British navy, who was celebrated for "cutting out" the French corvette *La Tapageuse* off the coast of France in 1806.

When Sutherland's body was recovered it was ceremonially transported to the flour shed next to the station by six sailors — and then draped with the Union Jack.

James Sutherland's two brothers were both mariners and both drowned at sea. He too drowned — in a few feet of murky water beneath the Desjardins Canal Bridge.

Why Sutherland, whose residence was in Hamilton, went to Toronto the day of the accident is not known. He was accompanied on the train by Edward Duffield, another Hamiltonian and mate of the steamer *Europa*. Some mutual business interest could have been what brought them together, or just plain conviviality. They were accompanied to the station by well-known Toronto sailor Captain

Henry Twohy. Whether business, pleasure, or both had brought the group together, they were clearly loath to separate. Apparently on a whim, Twohy was convinced to travel to Hamilton and spend the night with his friends. He boarded the train and took a seat in the deadly first car beside Sutherland. He later claimed that as he chatted with his friends a feeling came over him that he should not leave Toronto — a sort of presentment of evil. Whether his change of heart was driven by the spirit world or the loosening hand of the world of spirits cannot now be known. What is known is that he shook his friend's hands and announced: "On reflection, I will postpone my trip, as I have something to do at home." Four days later Twohy was one of the pallbearers who carried Captain Sutherland to his grave.

CHAPTER SIX

GREAT WESTERN RAILWAY:
FINANCIAL FITS AND STARTS

The railway age is popularly believed to have started with the opening of the first public steam railway along the twelve miles separating the English towns of Stockton and Darlington in 1825. Of course, like most technological "giant leaps" that landmark event was founded on decades, even centuries, of evolution. Precursors of the railway can be seen in the parallel ribbons of paved paths set about four feet apart that constituted a number of stone roads in Roman Britain. By the late 1700s European miners were moving coal and ore in horse-drawn trains along cast-iron flanged railways. As early as 1818 a tramway was in operation between the coal mines and the wharf at Pictou, Nova Scotia. Within five years of the Stockton and Darlington inauguration, railways had developed to embody all the main characteristics that are still associated with them today. When the first railway explicitly designed to carry passenger traffic opened between Liverpool and Manchester in 1830, it operated regularly between purpose-built stations, was exclusively steam hauled, and explicitly excluded access to its tracks by other carriers.

The innovation quickly leapfrogged the Atlantic. By 1830 the Camden and Amboy Railroad and Transportation Company had been chartered — not the first American railway, but the first to meet all the criteria of a commercial carrier. Although the prospectus for Canada's first railway was issued in 1832, it was late in 1834 before the Champlain and St. Lawrence Railway was formally organized, and it was not until 1836 that the line's first steam locomotive arrived from the Newcastle upon Tyne firm of Robert Stephenson & Company. After some initial teething problems the locomotive Dorchester proved a modest success. Shuttling back and forth between La Prairie, on the south shore of the St. Lawrence opposite Montreal, to Saint-Jean on the Richelieu River (a distance of just under fifteen miles), the line proved a boon to travellers and commerce between New York and Montreal. The shortcut prevented traffic travelling north of Lake Champlain from having to pass up the Richelieu to the St. Lawrence and then travel upstream to Montreal, a saving of almost a hundred miles.

Railways constructed to shorten the distance between two bodies of water were known as portage railways — for obvious reasons. In a country where ice closed all but the largest lakes to navigation for much of the year, and where rapids and waterfalls made many routes impractical throughout the entire year, the potential for portage railways in Canada was immediately clear. One of the progenitors of the Great Western was just such a line.

The idea of the Great Western predates Canadian Confederation by more than a third of a century. The seed of the scheme was sown even before Upper and Lower Canada were united into the Province of Canada. In 1832, when the entire population between Hamilton, at the head of Lake Ontario, and the Detroit River numbered less than 70,000, the residents of London petitioned the Upper Canadian legislature to permit the incorporation of a railway company to construct an iron or wooden railway from that city to the head of Lake Ontario. At that early date, railways were decidedly in their infancy. The initial enthusiasm of the Londoners took a couple of years to translate into a charter, and almost two decades passed before material progress could be demonstrated.

Still, the incorporation of the London and Gore Railway on March 6, 1834, marked the formal beginnings of the Great Western. Among the seventy signatories to the act of incorporation was Allan Napier MacNab, the future "father" of the Great Western.

Although born in the "new world," MacNab was a patrician of the old school. By right of birth he was Laird of the MacNab clan — a fiery tribe based in Perthshire, Scotland, whose fortunes, despite a reputation for bravery and expansion, had rarely been translated into material wealth. By the 1830s MacNab had firmly established a legal practice in the Gore District (which comprised the city of Hamilton and the surrounding countryside, as much as sixty miles distant). In the 1828 election MacNab won the local riding — outmaneuvering James Hamilton, the aging and increasingly distant city founder.

The Honourable Sir Allan Napier MacNab, the "Laird of Dundurn Castle," played a key role in the construction of the Great Western Railway during the 1830s to the 1850s. Throughout the various stops and starts that characterized construction, MacNab served as promoter, president, and chair of the railway committee that oversaw legislation. In this badly damaged photo, the elderly MacNab is pictured with his daughters and their Aunt Sophia.

COURTESY OF DUNDURN NATIONAL HISTORIC SITE.

In much the same way that the colossal commercial influence of Samuel Zimmerman has been mysteriously expunged from memory, Sir Allan Napier MacNab has been relegated to footnote status in Canada's political development. Canadian history is typically dated to 1867. In reality, the country's political foundation was formed a quarter-of-a-century before Confederation with the union of Upper and Lower Canada into a single province called Canada, with administrative divisions named Canada West and Canada East. John A. Macdonald, as every Canadian student is reminded, was Canada's first prime minister. But he assumed that position before Confederation as prime minister of the Canadian Union (in those days the title "premier" and "prime minister" were used interchangeably). His predecessor was Allan MacNab, and John A. was one of Sir Allan's political lieutenants. MacNab's role in the country's development deserves wider recognition.

That is not to suggest that MacNab merits veneration as a benevolent leader shepherding an emerging economic force toward nationhood. Like most politicians of the time, his main interest was parlaying his position and status into financial advantage. In that regard he was a noteworthy analog of his younger contemporary Zimmerman, but by all accounts a more arrogant and less flamboyant personality.

As a member of the legislature, MacNab was in a position to advance the railway's interests. As a director of the railway he was positioned to benefit from the railway's construction — even if the line itself proved unprofitable. Such an obvious conflict evoked little criticism in nineteenth-century Upper Canada. It was understood and accepted that office was sought to further personal gain and that the ensuing industrial expansion served to bolster the fortunes of the community at large.

At those early days of their history, railways were conceived as ways of joining two locations. That individual lines might one day be interconnected to form a transportation network was not recognized. Often the early lines were intended as a means of circumventing an obstacle to navigation, such as Niagara Falls. That mighty barrier constituted the primary reason behind proposals for the London and Gore Railway. The Great Lakes constituted a gigantic navigation system that could open up the vast interior of North America for development. Yet the Falls effectively barred navigation and precluded expansion. True, the obstacle had been circumvented by the Welland Canal in Canada, and in the United States by the Erie Canal system linking Lake Erie through the Hudson River to New York. But canals froze in the winter — and winters then were longer and harsher than they are today. The London and Gore was a prime example of a "portage" railway, designed as a sort of land bridge from London on the Thames River to the head of Lake Ontario.

Where the eastern terminus of the railway was to be was not entirely clear. There are indications that the town of Dundas was the preferred place. Today, Dundas is a tranquil suburb on the shores of a marshy lake called Cootes Paradise, a few miles west of the vastly larger and heavily industrial city of Hamilton. But in the early decades of the 1800s it was Dundas, with its access to water power from the many stream that plunge over the conspicuous Niagara Escarpment, that had the upper hand. Even a committee of the House of Assembly opined "while Hamilton enjoyed a viable future, it was unlikely ever to rival Dundas!"

A terminus at Dundas might have seemed like an attractive proposition for MacNab. Only a few years earlier a short passage had been cut through the narrow strip of land across the mouth of Burlington Bay, providing Hamilton with the finest harbour on all the Great Lakes. Dundas was separated from that harbour only by the shallow fen of Cootes Paradise, and plans were afoot to dredge a ten-foot-deep channel through it to the navigable water of the bay.

That project — the very same canal into which the Great Western train plunged — had been commenced by Peter Dejardins in 1826. On his death, less than two years later, construction halted. Unsuccessful efforts were made to revitalize the scheme but it was not until there was stronger financial backing and a new and aggressive president took the corporate reins that significant progress began to take place. That president was none other than Allan MacNab.

While MacNab's interests in the Desjardins Canal might suggest a motive for preferring Dundas as the terminus of the Great Western, it was probably under his influence that, when the necessary act was passed, the company's charter specified "the harbour on Burlington Bay" as the end of line. The reason that MacNab would favour Hamilton is easy to understand. A very large portion of the land and buildings in Hamilton were owned by him. Since MacNab's arrival in Hamilton in 1826 the city had caught up with Dundas, and by 1832 Hamilton had a population of around eight hundred, almost two hundred more citizens than Dundas. The construction of a rail link would further the economic pace and certainly inflate property prices — and no one would benefit more than MacNab.

To cement his position as Hamilton's most prominent leader, in 1833 Allan MacNab — lawyer, financier, developer — acquired possibly the choicest residential location in Upper Canada. The Beasley Tract stood at the northern fringe of the city on the strip of high land that separates Burlington Bay and Cootes Paradise. A strategic camp during the War of 1812, the Burlington Heights on which the property sits enjoys a commanding view of the bay to the east. To the west, Cootes Paradise was a veritable paradise of wildlife — and MacNab loved fishing and shooting more than he loved the law. At the northern end of the heights, where the ancient dike had succumbed to the stream draining Dundas Valley, the Desjardins Canal snaked around the headland. On this spot MacNab constructed an astonishing seventy-two-room mansion called Dundurn Castle — named for the Scottish seat of the MacNab clan. The Laird had arrived!

MacNab's intense involvement with both the canal and the railway seem eerily reflected in his decision to locate his estate on this stretch of high ground. Eventually the Desjardins Canal would be relocated through a steep cutting at the border of his property. The Great Western would be routed into Hamilton below the windows of his mansion, at his insistence, on lakefront land he sold to the railway. The catastrophic accident that connected the railway and the canal could, in fact, have been witnessed from the Laird's incredible manor.

But when the London and Gore act was passed in 1832 all of that was in the future. The Desjardins Canal was not completed until 1837, and even then was navigable only for boats drawing seven and a half feet. Within a few years it had silted-in to only five feet. And the railway? That too was struggling through difficult times. A bevy of competing railway schemes were being proposed — among them a short loop around Niagara Falls that was actually constructed in 1839, but the ruling gradients were too steep for the primitive locomotives available and traffic had to be hauled by horse.

This rare photograph shows the British directors of the Great Western gathered on the lawn outside Dundurn Castle. The legend identifies some of those present: Alan MacNab is just to the right of the two ladies in white. Also included are Isaac Buchanan (no. 4); C.W. Brydges, manager of the GTR (no. 14); and George Reid, the engineer (no. 15).

COURTESY OF DUNDURN CASTLE HISTORIC SITE.

Still, the London and Gore had failed to raise the modest £100,000 necessary to consider construction. By 1836 a Rochester, New York, engineer, Elisha Johnson, had been hired to conduct a preliminary survey. His fees were largely met out of pocket by MacNab and a handful of other directors. His findings were enthusiastic — even theatrical. They served well as evidence before a select committee of the assembly, fortuitously chaired by none other than Allan MacNab himself.

While railway politics had degenerated into a series of mutual accommodations to appease the myriad schemes being promoted by a multiplicity of interests, MacNab was able to marshal through the committee and eventually the assembly amended the charter in 1837. This new charter changed the name of the company to the Great Western Rail Road, gave it powers to run between Hamilton and the Michigan border, expanded its capital, and provided for a public loan of £200,000. The news was so enthusiastically received in Hamilton that, in a short space of time, land prices in that city jumped by 50 percent — a phenomenon that must have deeply warmed MacNab's acquisitive heart.

But the promised funds were never delivered. The unsettled colonial politics unleashed the rebellion of 1837. In Upper Canada, diminutive William Lyon Mackenzie and his supporters proposed a Canadian republic and actively sought U.S. support. William Lyon Mackenzie, having vowed to take Toronto by force, was ignominiously routed at Montgomery's Tavern on the city's Yonge Street after a half-hour battle — a manoeuvre in which MacNab, as colonel of the militia, played a very prominent role. Although the rebellion in both Lower and Upper Canada were not long lasting, their repercussions dramatically altered the politics of British North America, ultimately leading to political union.

In light of MacNab's patriotic leadership during the Upper Canadian Rebellion, Britain's "Iron Duke," the Duke of Wellington (of Waterloo fame), came to refer to MacNab as the "right arm of British power in North America."

Great Western Railway: Financial Fits and Starts

When Mackenzie and his followers fled Toronto they made their way to Niagara, where they set up a camp on Navy Island. Once ensconced, they continued to thumb their noses at the authorities. MacNab and his "men of Gore" pursued them to the bank of the Niagara River, where a standoff ensued.

The rebels appeared to be safely barricaded with a clear line of shot against any small boats that might venture to approach them from the Canadian side. More to the point, American authorities on the other side of the river were tacitly supporting and actively supplying the rebels. With British-American relations strained, Governor Bond Head was anxious to avoid confrontation and the militia was under orders of restraint. When the American supply vessel *Caroline* was reactivated from her winter moorings during the early days of January 1838, and seen ferrying armaments to the rebels from New York State, it looked as if the rebels would become entrenched. On witnessing the unloading of a cannon on the island, MacNab observed to one of his officers: "I say, Drew, this won't do. Do you think you can cut out that boat?" The confident answer was that it could easily be accomplished after dark.

Whether deliberately or recklessly, MacNab's forces probably brought Canada and the United States closer to war than they had been since the War of 1812, or than they have been since. The *Caroline* was expected to be moored for the night on Navy Island. When the small raiding party went looking for her, however, they found her tied up on the U.S. shore. They attacked, routing the crew and killing one American. The *Caroline* was set afire and left to drift down the rapid current toward the Falls.

When word of the exploit became known, the citizens of nearby Buffalo were incensed. Talk of armed retribution was widespread. But no intervention ensued and the success emboldened authorities to mount a more aggressive campaign against the rebels. By the time this was conducted, weeks later, it was discovered to the chagrin of the authorities that the island's apparently substantial barricades were of little consequence and the rebels had quietly slipped into the United States.

On the strength of his patriotic exploits in Toronto and, in particular, his audacious destruction of the American *Caroline*, MacNab became a wildly popular hero. MacNab, no shrinking violet, revelled in the praise — reaching a point of ecstasy when, in March 1838, Queen Victoria knighted him for his services. Sir Allan Napier MacNab gloried in his newfound rank. His irascible cynicism, however, is evident in his scribbled addendum to a copy of the Legislative Assembly's approbatory address: "Not worth a fart!"

A knight of the realm, an honoured military leader, an influential politician, and a local hero — MacNab was all of these in 1838. But successful businessman and railway developer he was not. The Gore Bank, which he had helped establish, had extended him considerable credit, under more favourable terms than many felt justified. Charges of fraud and inflated property sales swirled around MacNab. Heavily mortgaged, before the decade was out he was obliged to forfeit some of his property when the Bank of Upper Canada seized and sold it.

For railway construction, whether funded privately or publicly, the political turmoil of the latter 1830s were not propitious times — compounding, as they did, the consequences of a severe economic recession that was engulfing North America. Several disastrous harvests in Canada and the United States, accompanied by sharp falls in commodity prices and the collapse of unsustainable railway manias in Europe and the United States, meant hard times for all — especially capital-deficient colonial rail lines. The newly chartered Great Western slipped back into dormancy.

By 1843 the North American economic slump was ending. Promoters not only foresaw better prospects of attracting capital, but recognized a whole new rationale for railway construction. Railways were no longer perceived as portage roads or simple routes joining two cities. The Great Western was being promoted as a strategic link in at least two grand schemes. By the mid-1840s American railroads connected Boston and New York with Buffalo. The gap between Detroit and Chicago was almost bridged. The route of the

Great Western Railway: Financial Fits and Starts

Great Western offered a significantly shorter and easier path between Buffalo and Detroit than any alternative route through New York State on the southern side of Lake Erie. Tapping the burgeoning traffic of the American Midwest bound for the U.S. eastern seaboard would make the Great Western a very viable proposition indeed.

The railway was also well situated to deliver both Canadian and American goods for transshipment to the lower-Great Lakes/St. Lawrence River navigation system. As the decade wore on, however, an even more agreeable possibility began to take shape.

Initiatives got underway to build a rail connection between Montreal and the seaport of Portland, Maine. The St. Lawrence and Atlantic Railway, along with its U.S. counterpart the Atlantic and St. Lawrence, would provide Montreal and all traffic passing through that city with a year-round outlet on the ocean — unaffected by seasonal freezes. Of course, it took only a little imagination to recognize that an additional line linking Montreal and Toronto and points to the west, along the easy gradients bordering Lake Ontario, would be highly attractive to traffic from both Upper Canada and the American Midwest. Add the possibility that the contemplated Intercolonial Railway would be constructed to link Halifax and Montreal, and the Great Western could instantly hold a highly strategic position in the Canadian "grand trunk line" that was being talked about.

Thus, the Great Western proposal held three strong cards. It represented a key shortcut for American traffic between the Mississippi, Chicago and the Midwest, and the ports of New York and Boston. It could play an integral role in the Canadian Grand Trunk scheme — possibly funnelling goods from the west of the continent to the ports of Montreal, Halifax, and Portland. Finally, it would serve a rich agricultural and manufacturing basin in Upper Canada, which lay partially locked behind the barrier of the Niagara Falls. In the period since the London and Gore had been first mooted, an area that had experienced astronomical population growth along with economic expansion and diversity.

END OF THE LINE

* * *

A short digression may be appropriate at this point to explain what lay behind this phenomenal explosion of railroad expansion in North America. During the early years of the nineteenth century the population of the continent was concentrated along the eastern seaboard and the navigable shores of rivers such as the St. Lawrence. The immense potential of the North American interior was widely recognized, but existing transport routes were simply too primitive to allow exploitation. That began to change dramatically with the arrival of the short-lived canal era. In 1825 the Erie Canal was opened, linking Lake Erie with New York through the Hudson River. A few years later the first Welland Canal provided navigation around Niagara Falls on the Canadian side.

These developments encouraged a major influx into the region. The population of Upper Canada (today's Ontario) was around 71,000 in 1806. By 1825 it had more than doubled, to 158,000. But that was only the beginning. The introduction of the railroad made the canals almost obsolete overnight. As disconnected projects spread out into the centre of the continent, the rush to complete links and create networks turned into frenzy. During that period, Americans, many of them entrepreneurs and professionals, flowed into Upper Canada, swelling the earlier wave of United Empire Loyalists, and European immigrants flooded in, attracted by available land and glowing economic prospects. By 1832 the population had exploded to more than a quarter of a million, and by 1848 had more than doubled again. By the time the Great Western was finally brought into service, Upper Canada — or Canada West as it had become — was home to almost one million.

While the population was expanding more than ten-fold in a few short decades, society was maturing from pioneer settlements into respectable towns and cities. While many remained dependent upon hard physical labour for their livelihood, others were becoming wealthy and acquiring all the trappings of the rich — substantial mansions, large domestic staff, and extensive travel. The introduction of steam-driven ocean liners made international travel a comfortable prospect. Many of the political and commercial elite of the mid-1800s were able to voyage to distant, even exotic, locations almost as a matter of routine. Of course, industry was being revolutionized. Waterpower was giving way to steam power — no longer constrained by location. New modes of transport were vastly expanding markets and technology was exploding.

Small wonder that in July 1845 the lapsed charter of the London and Gore was resurrected. The new act provided for the name to be changed to the Great Western Railroad and powers were granted for the line to run from the Niagara River to the St. Clair River, passing through Hamilton along the way. All but one of the new board of directors were Hamilton based. The president was none other than Sir Allan Napier MacNab.

The first concern had to be the raising of sufficient capital to get the project underway. Local funds were thinly stretched. U.S. financiers were by then well seasoned in railroad matters — with myriad lines proposed and already constructed in that country. While relations had certainly improved, tensions between Canada and the United States were still fresh and American capital was viewed somewhat unfavourably. In Britain, however, there had been a veritable explosion of railway promotion and yet it seemed there were never too many prospectuses to satisfy the fever.

In the autumn of 1845 Sir Allan travelled to Britain. In a whirlwind of activity he had sewn up financing in a matter of days. The Buchanan family (originally from Glasgow, Scotland) had established commercial operations in Glasgow, London, New York, Montreal, and Hamilton. MacNab's first course was to contact Peter Buchanan in Glasgow. Buchanan hastily travelled to London and introduced MacNab to unquestioned "Railway King" George Hudson. Hudson's aura was such that the mere suspicion of his interest in a scheme could add pounds to its share price overnight.

Hudson and a group of very influential London businessmen agreed to form a corresponding committee to oversee the placement of 55,000 of the 60,000 authorized shares in British hands. Despite reservations concerning many Canadian railway issues, British investors rapidly priced the issue at a strong premium. The first three calls on the stock were eagerly paid and the Great Western Railway was at last in a position to contemplate construction.

It was not to be. Yet again the scheme faltered. With a substantial allotment of the British shares made to himself as agent, and having acquired a significant number of the Canadian shares of the Great Western, MacNab sailed back to Canada thinking the transactions had made him, as Peter Buchanan had suggested, "a thoroughly independent man in pecuniary matters." Before he reached home, the Bank of England had raised interest rates, and the stock market collapsed. Worse, the corresponding committee, greedy to reserve the greater part of the stocks' anticipated appreciation for themselves, had placed only a modest proportion of the shares with the public. There was talk of folding the enterprise before the first sod had even been turned.

What followed was an inglorious period of squabbling, backbiting, and connivance that drew in politicians, financiers, and developers alike. In short, nineteenth century railway politics were being conducted according to the accustomed standards of morality. MacNab, under personal attack and having experienced recent poor health as well as the death of his sickly wife, declared: "I never was so miserable in my life — I would not go through all I have done here for any consideration."

Sir Allan's personal despondency had not rendered him inactive. By the spring of 1846 he had used his unquestioned lobby powers in the assembly (along with some £1,000 of the corresponding committee's reluctant money) to rewrite the Great Western's charter, giving it the power to construct railways between Hamilton and Toronto, and Toronto and Kingston, as well as the right to absorb the Kingston and Montreal Railway. With this promise of enviously broad powers in hand, by the end of that year Sir Allan was able to

Great Western Railway: Financial Fits and Starts

hammer out a new arrangement with the British backers, solidifying their commitment and bringing in some material finance.

More money was desperately required, but efforts to place stock in Canada and the United States had yielded paltry results. An effort was made to interest the British government in advancing a very substantial loan in support of a scheme whereby impoverished Scots and Irish would be imported to build the line and ultimately settled on railway land. Nothing came of it.

Enough capital was raised to complete the preliminary survey by the fall of 1847 and, armed with details suggesting even easier gradients, shorter distances, and straighter rights of way than earlier anticipated, contracts were let and construction, of a sort, got underway.

On October 23, 1847, some 3,000 spectators witnessed Thomas Talbot turn the first sod in London. The shops were closed, the forces and organizations paraded, and the town celebrated. The jubilation was short-lived. Economic conditions were already beginning to deteriorate yet again, and political strife was manifest. Work on the railway stagnated.

In the summer of 1847 the wheat market collapsed. Banks began to call their loans and Sir Allan, who had constantly been pushing his debt limit in order to acquire more and more land, was severely strapped — creditors were even threatening to seize the contents of his precious castle.

Although notionally united into the single Province of Canada by the 1840 act, the colony was still heavily split on linguistic grounds. The election of 1848 saw the routing of MacNab's Tory party (although Sir Allan kept his seat and remained party leader) and the ascendancy of the reform party. "Reform" stood less for the reform of government practices than for the reform of government answerability. The objective of the movement was to achieve "responsible government" — i.e., to diminish the powers of the colonial governor and make him responsible to the will of the people.

In 1849 English-speaking Tory radicals in Montreal, angered by the governor's signing of a bill providing compensating for damages resulting from the 1837 rebellion, burned out the House of Assembly, which was housed within the market (to which it had relocated from Kingston in 1844). Although unable to save the precious library, Sir Allan and others were able to preserve from the flames the painting of Queen Victoria, which today hangs prominently in the Parliament Buildings in Ottawa.

The last year of that decade saw the introduction of two crucial pieces of legislation that carried the promise of a cash infusion into railways. Under the direction of Francis Hincks, the Reform prime minister, the Guarantee Act and the Municipal Act opened access to public funds. Under the terms of the former, the province would guarantee the interest at 6 percent on the debt of any railway seventy-five miles in length, once it was at least half completed. Under the second, municipalities were empowered to own stock in and to lend to railways.

While on a return trip Britain, attempting to wring further financial concessions from the recalcitrant corresponding committee, MacNab found himself undermined from within his own board. One of the directors, George Tiffany, had succeeded in having MacNab's devalued Great Western stock seized and sold by the sheriff. While he remained on as a director, the sale meant that MacNab was no longer qualified to act as president. Robert Harris was elected in his place. Sir Allan relapsed into personal despondency, but still fought hard for the Great Western. He knew that the railway's success was his only real hope of reaping the rewards of his huge land speculations.

The years during which Sir Allan exercised direct control over the administration of the Great Western had been marked by a great deal of discord. There were numerous charges of mismanagement and self-serving — many of which must have been largely justified. At the insistence of Sir Allan the railway was routed via the northern side of Dundas Valley. While that route facilitated the extension of the line into Toronto, it entailed far greater engineering demands than would have an easier approach to Hamilton along the southern side. It also required crossing Burlington Heights, the eventual rerouting of the Desjardins Canal, the construction of the notorious bridge, and the purchase, from Sir Allan, of the strip of waterfront property below his castle — a substantial portion of which was actually under the lake!

Perversely, it is probably when he was no longer at the helm of the company that he made his greatest contribution to the eventual success of the enterprise. Sir Allan never made a lot of money out of the Great Western, but his fortunes were well and truly vested in Hamilton. Rival railway schemes would have centred their operations elsewhere. Proponents of the "northern" route would strike a path from Toronto to the St. Clair River. The much-touted "southern" route would connect Niagara directly to Detroit, bypassing Hamilton.

Sir Allan's strong support of locally based initiatives served to get him re-elected time after time in Hamilton, despite the often chameleon-like nature of his politics. A one-time member of the Family Compact, patrician Sir Allan would eventual seek the recall of Governor Lord Elgin. A "high Tory," MacNab defended the Montreal

A modern photograph of Dundurn Castle, taken in 2009. MacNab's magnificent seventy-two-room mansion bespeaks his flamboyant style of living — despite his frequent brushes with insolvency. The castle and grounds are open to the public.
COURTESY OF RICK CORDEIRA.

Parliament against radical Tory attackers. Despite a poor command of French, he coveted and attained the position of speaker in the assembly. A self-interestedly passionate promoter of Upper Canadian interests, MacNab happily engineered strategic alliances with French-Canadian politicians. Those conveniences scarcely mattered — he was famously reported as claiming that all his politics were railroads and he would support whoever supported railroads. In his influential political position as chairman of the Standing Committee on Railways and Telegraphs, Sir Allan best served the interests of the Great Western.

The Municipal Act of 1849, permitting localities to provide direct loans to railways, opened a veritable flood of subscriptions from towns anxious to see their constituents benefit commercially from railway proximity. The towns of London and Galt, as well as the counties of Middlesex and Oxford, promptly anted up £25,000 each in favour of the Great Western. Hamilton, under the urging of Mayor Colin Ferrie, was on the verge of buying in to the extent of £100,000, until it was pointed out that such a huge amount exceed the city's total assessment. A more modest £50,000 was paid. This over extension of municipal credit placed an onerous burden on municipalities. The city of Hamilton eventually became bankrupt, and by 1862 seventy-six out of seventy-eight that had subscribed to various railway schemes were in default. The end result was that the province had to assume municipal debt.

The measures were, of course, not aimed specifically toward the Great Western. Hincks's main objective was to obtain financing for the more audacious main Grand Trunk scheme that would unite Montreal with Detroit and with the U.S. eastern seaboard and, quite possibly, the Canadian east coast. When the Guarantee Act was brought in the Great Western was perceived as an integral link in the larger scheme. Even when the act was revised in 1851, to allow its benefits to apply solely to railways constructed as part of the main trunk line, the Great Western was explicitly included in the legislation.

Great Western Railway: Financial Fits and Starts

If Allan MacNab could claim to be the father of the Great Western, Francis Hincks was undoubtedly destined to prove its spoiler. Born in Ireland in 1807, he settled in Canada in the early 1830s with a commercial background. In 1841 he entered politics and rose quickly to the highest elected position in Canada. Hincks was a suave and effective negotiator — as capable of pleading his case within the upper echelons of the British government as within his own caucus. His years in banking gave him the capacity to deal with international financiers, as if he was one of the club. And he always kept a close eye to his own interest. Hincks was no more cursed with an overactive sense of morality than were many of his colleagues.

Hincks earned the nickname the Hyena. While he was initially enthusiastic about the Great Western's inclusion in the government-sponsored Grand Trunk, when the act granting the Grand Trunk's charter was introduced all mention of the Great Western had been dropped. The Grand Trunk was to strike for the shore of the St. Clair independently, via the northern route. Strategic alliances with Montreal and Toronto interests essentially resulted in the Great Western being left competing for the traffic it had thought it would monopolize.

Perhaps more damning still, the Hincks government insisted that railways applying for the government guarantee would have to satisfy the technical requirements specified by the Board of Railway Commissioners. They mandated that the gauge of the railway would have to conform to the Provincial Gauge of five feet, six inches, that the St. Lawrence and Atlantic and its American counterpart had adopted, in order to prevent the loss of their traffic to competing U.S. lines. The Grand Trunk, which intended to incorporate the St. Lawrence and Atlantic, naturally selected the same gauge. The Great Western was planning on a gauge of four feet, eight and a half inches. While there were still a plethora of different size tracks in the United States, railway networks were increasingly gravitating to the so-called "standard gauge." In fact, in 1851 the Great Western had been able to attract a million-dollar investment by Erasmus Corning on behalf of the New York Central System on the explicit promise of adopting that gauge.

Corning declared the Great Western was a vital link in an American "grand trunk route," linking the Atlantic and the Mississippi.

The Great Western was in a bind. It could not afford to pass up the government guarantee, but adopting it would severely compromise the railway's value as a seamless transfer point between the two big American systems in New York and Michigan.

The loss of trunk status in both Canada and the United States was a bitter pill. But, cosseted with conditions as they were, avenues of finance were becoming available. Municipal subscriptions were flowing in. The board was able to mollify the American investors over the change in gauge, keeping funds flowing. Contracts were let in 1851, and the contractors agreed to take up to $800,000 in par stock as partial payment.

Financing the Great Western was in many ways as monumental a task as the physical job of actually constructing the line. While construction occupied the lives of thousands, finance could only be secured by the diligence of a few sophisticated and technically adept proponents. Vast funds were often controlled by a handful of capitalists. Major schemes could be agreed on by a small number of men, comfortably ensconced in leather armchairs sipping expensive brandy. But men did not achieve such financial power without knowing the value of their own money. There was no philanthropy in railway finance! Funds were invested only after a shrewd assessment of the worth of the project and the reputation of its champions. Between the first contemplation of a rail link between London and Hamilton and the start of serious construction almost two decades had passed. People like Sir Allan had progressed from early middle age to approaching retirement. During those years of waxing and waning fortunes, Sir Allan frequently complained of the hours dedicated to furthering the railway, hours spent writing letters, eliciting support, and rebutting objections. Days, weeks, and months spent badgering fellow members of the assembly and lobbying the influential. Monies spent on intermediaries and agents to maintain interest, and even bribes paid to achieve objectives.

"The Hyena," Sir Francis Hincks was at various times both benefactor and ultimate spoiler of the Great Western, depending on which way his political and financial fortunes blew. But he always remained a good friend of Sam Zimmerman. Hinks left Canadian politics to become governor, first of Barbados, and then of British Guiana. During his terms in the Caribbean he became a strong opponent of slavery on economic grounds.

MCCORD MUSEUM, WILLIAM NOTMAN 1873, I88358.

Perhaps Sir Allan and his contemporaries complained too much. The affairs of finance certainly occupied a lot of time and required a singleness of purpose — but there were perks. Our visions of pre-Confederation Canada may have become distorted by the rapid advances of technology, science, and communication that seem so much more a phenomenon of the twentieth century rather than the nineteenth. Our view of the 1850s may be one in which few ventured more than a few miles from their birthplace, in which travel was constrained to sleighs in winter and springless carts bumping along boggy cordwood roads in summer. As we have already seen, the reality was very different.

The burgeoning industrial world was a beehive of mobility. Huge migrations from impoverished parts of Europe (notably Ireland) were underway, bringing agriculturists and artisans to settle the hinterlands. Railways, as they expanded, rapidly offered transportation not merely to the elite but to the common person. Living standards were dramatically improving. While hardly typical of average conditions, Sir Allan's magnificent castle boasted indoor plumbing and central heating. The steamship offered predictable passage between Europe and North America, and the railways provided comfortable transportation to the seaports. While far from commonplace, transatlantic travel for the leading citizens had become at least unremarkable by the 1850s, and the steamship companies were vying with each other to provide greater and greater luxuries for the first-class salon traveller.

Globalization is no modern phenomenon. The Great Western was headquartered in Canada but planned as an international service. The majority shareholders and bondholders were British — with some participation by American corporations. The contractors were American and Canadian. The construction workforce was multi-national, with a significant Irish contingent. Free trade was in its ascendancy in the mid-1800s. Britain had abandoned the Imperial Preference that had provided favourable treatment of colonial exporters, and Canada and the United States were discussing trade reciprocity. The locomotives for the Great Western were imported from the United States and from Britain. The rails themselves also came from Britain.

In early summer 1855 the *Hamilton Spectator* reported without particular comment that Francis Hincks and William Cayley (MacNab's finance minister) were en route to the United Kingdom, where they would be joined by Sir Allan and John A. Macdonald. The foursome would then travel on to Paris to visit the World's Fair. That rather casual notice highlights two realities of the time. The first: cutthroat business dealings by no means precluded the enjoyment of mutual pleasures. The second: transatlantic crossings were becoming routine.

While contemporary observers marvelled at the ability to shuttle between New York and London in a mere ten to fifteen days by steam (in contrast with the unpredictable weeks required by sail), there was still no other means of overseas communication than the mails. U.S. legislation enabling the first short-lived attempt to lay a submarine telegraph was actually signed by the president just days before the Desjardins Canal catastrophe. But it was not until the Royal Mail steamer *Persia* docked in Liverpool, two weeks later, that news of the tragedy reached London. A scattering of detail appeared in *The Times of London* on March 30th, forwarded by telegraph from Liverpool. Prominent in the few short paragraphs of that report was the news that "Mr. S. Zimmerman, the wealthy contractor and banker of Niagara, is among the victims."

Although the Great Western was to remain independent for another quarter century, the Desjardins catastrophe coincided with the company's highpoint. The early years of operation proved remarkably rewarding. Revenues substantially exceeded expectations and the company was able to regularly pay generous dividends of 6 to 8 percent or more, and established a sinking fund that provided for the orderly repayment of government loans. In contrast, the Grand Trunk returned time and again to the public trough — an early example of that almost uniquely Canadian phenomenon: the publicly funded megaproject. Like later manifestations of the ilk, the government was too deeply entangled to allow the Grand Trunk to fail. The old adage that owing the bank a million dollars meant you were in trouble, while owing the bank a hundred million dollars meant the bank was in trouble, was proven in the affairs of the Great Western. When deteriorating prospects brought it knocking at government's door it was largely ignored, while the Grand Trunk received continuing support and ultimately subsumed the Great Western.

The disaster itself was not what triggered the dwindling fortunes of the Great Western. Rebuilding the bridge involved only moderate expenditure, and the loss of a few cars and even the wrecking of the locomotive were little more than operating expenses to the railway. Accident liabilities in the 1850s were vastly less onerous than they are for modern corporations. While the Great Western did pay out a total of £29,000 sterling in compensation in 1857, that amount was only about three times what it was for the preceding and ensuing years. While that amounted to about 10 percent of expenditure in 1857, one should bear in mind the shocking safety record of the company — about which more details are given in the following chapter. Still, in 1857 the Great Western was able to pay a dividend of 5.75 percent — although it withheld repayment on the government loan.

If one believes William Lyon Mackenzie, the company even managed to turn the disaster to its own good — charging relatives for the transport of the victims remains and even levying a four dollar fee for each of the simple pine boxes in which they were shipped. Mind you, one would be ill-advised to take Mackenzie charges at face value. The erstwhile rebel, long since restored to public office, was somewhat of a professional malcontent whose explosive sense of injury was often fuelled by strong drink. Ever since Sir Allan MacNab had been so instrumental in foiling Mackenzie's ill-considered efforts to become the first president of the Canadian Republic, McKenzie had had no love for Sir Allan and every interest in denigrating the Great Western. While accepting that the Great Western suffered multitudinous deficiencies in construction and management, Mackenzie's charges of connivance and perfidy against company officials concerning the condition of the bridge seem more than a little intemperate.

The disaster — and even the chain of catastrophes — did not play much of a role in the demise of the Great Western. Once again economic fortunes shifted. In 1858 a North-America-wide recession slashed the revenues of major railroad companies by as much as 25 percent. The Great Western fared better than many, slumping only 13 percent. But expenditures were still under upward pressure as improvement and replacement of the crudely built infrastructure became ever more urgent. Bridges needed to be rebuilt, track re-laid, rails replaced, and rolling stock constantly maintained against the viscous effects of the rough riding and defective road. By 1859 the company could declare no dividend at all.

For the balance of its history the railway was on a downward spiral. There were periods of expansion and returning optimism, but after each bout of ill fortune the Great Western faced increasing competition. The Grand Trunk continued to maintain a government-bolstered advantage to the north, while to the south the Southern Railway, blessed by the most famous of the American railway barons, Cornelius Vanderbilt, diverted much of the traffic of the New York Central System away from the Great Western and onto its own "standard" gauge tracks.

The U.S. Civil War that commenced in 1861 had a major unsettling effect on investment in "British North America." The American traffic on which the Great Western had counted so much became financially risky. Between 1862 and 1869 the railway lost almost 20 percent of its gross earnings on through traffic to currency losses. Debased coinage and heavily discounted paper money cost the railway more than £800 sterling over the period.

In 1864 the railway recognized what it had suspected from the start — that competition with rival lines would not be possible until it converted to standard gauge. The conversion was completed by 1866, but not before the Great Western had expended a further urgently needed £700,000.

Eventually successive bouts of competition with the Grand Trunk and American competitors, as well as the battle to improve and maintain the quality of the line, took their toll. Revenues already depressed by a crop failure a couple of years earlier were severely curbed by ice in the Detroit River that blocked traffic for as long as two months. Currency instability resulted in a further bout of exchange losses — amounting to $300,000 in a single year. Another sharp recession hit the North American economy in 1873. Banks again withheld specie payment — issuing paper only. Commodity prices plummeted and bankruptcies rose.

By the 1880s the writing was on the wall. The Canadian Pacific Railway constituted a new transcontinental force with which the Great Western would have to deal with — either as ally or adversary. The Grand Trunk made its move. The thoroughly abused act of 1852 that had originally included the Great Western as part of the trunk route (the same that Hincks and his associates had conveniently ignored when the Grand Trunk was chartered) now provided an opportunity for the amalgamation of the two railways without the need for additional legislation. The Great Western board was not happy, but at a special meeting on June 29, 1882, the shareholders voted in favour of a Grand Trunk proposal, and the Great Western Railway of Canada passed into history.

For sheer audacity in the face of ceaseless challenge and treacherous scheming, the history of the Great Western must be viewed as heroic — but not triumphant.

CHAPTER SEVEN

GREAT WESTERN RAILWAY:
SHOVEL READY AT LAST

The most efficient railway to operate runs directly between two points with the fewest deviations possible and the easiest gradient that can be achieved. The builders of the earliest mainline railways in Britain respected those principles. The British Great Western Railway (of which the Great Western of Canada was a later namesake) connected London and Bristol by as direct a route as possible. Whenever Isambard Kingdom Brunel (the preposterously named yet most accomplished of the Victorian civil engineers) encountered an obstacle he tunneled through it or built over it. He could afford to. There was no competition in place or contemplated, and in any case the limited tractive power of the engines of the day made it essential to minimize the labour they would be called on to perform. Brunel's line was, and still is, a masterpiece of railway construction — straight and level with impressive tunnels, cuttings, and bridges.

When, only a short time later, the new technology made its North American debut, quite different economics came to the fore. Most of the early American lines were built through sparsely populated regions and encountered relatively severe physical barriers. The overarching objective was getting produce out and manufactured goods into the interior during the wet periods, when the crude land routes were impassable, and the many winter months, when the burgeoning canal system was closed. Speed was of secondary concern. Already locomotive design was advancing so that, while slipping sliding and wheezing, the machines could be driven over higher grades. Skirting obstacles was far cheaper than elaborate and expensive feats of engineering. The early American railroads were circuitous, poorly engineered, and accident prone, but they were effective and they were profitable.

Economic and geographic realities dictated construction techniques in North America. On lines without intermediate access to navigable water, all the equipment and whatever construction material that couldn't be wrested from the surrounding forest had to be brought in from one end or the other. To minimize that effort, some of the earliest lines were initially built using strap rail — a thin iron band, which formed the running surface, was spiked directly to wooden rails laid on wooden ties. When the surface would bear it, the initial track was frequently pegged to crossties laid directly on the crudely graded right-of-way. In the most extreme cases, track would be laid over frozen bogs or even across frozen lakes, all as a means of advancing equipment and material toward the end of line.

A great many of these enterprises were severely cash-strapped and until the line could be opened for traffic, not one cent of revenue could be generated. Standard practice was to open railroads well before they could in any way be considered completed. By restricting speed, tolerating lengthy delays, and resigning themselves to frequent derailments and even occasionally more serious accidents, the railroad companies could begin generating income, which was essential to pay for stabilizing the roadbed, building more permanent structures, and for eventual improvements to shorten routes and moderate the more severe gradients.

Canada's Great Western was constructed in precisely that manner. Like so many similar projects, it cost vastly more than originally estimated and, when opened, fell markedly short of the engineering specifications. More than that, it was notoriously unsafe. In 1854, on all the 8,000 miles of railway in operation in Britain, just twelve passengers were killed in accidents. That same year, operating on less than 250 miles, the Great Western managed to dispatch some seventy passengers to meet their maker! And that, of course, was three years before the tragedy at Desjardins.

Every event is the confluence of seemingly unrelated decisions made in the past, as the Desjardins disaster seems to exemplify. By what chance was the doomed train predestined to experience an axle failure at that exact time? By what fate was the Great Western line ordained to intersect the Canal — and why at that crucial location? Throughout so much of this complex tale, the paths of the Desjardins Canal and the Great Western Railway seem to constantly cross, both literally and figuratively. The superstitious might even discern a degree of predetermination. The two were, of course, linked through commercial interest and executive responsibility. Sir Allan, once president of the canal company, was also the prime force behind the Great Western, where he served as longtime director and president. Dr. Hamilton, another distinguished director of the railway at the time of the catastrophe, had by that time taken over the presidency of the canal company. Both men had interests that many strongly believed actually determined the location of where the two intersected — an unhappy selection that, had it been at any other point, might have prevented disaster. The decision was made to locate the railway along the northern side of Dundas Valley. Hamilton owned property along that flank that he hoped could be developed as a quarry; Sir Allan, of course, was anxious to sell the railway land adjacent to his Dundurn estate, upon which to build the terminus.

The path of the original survey of 1847 didn't specify bringing the line to the level of Lake Ontario at Hamilton. By the time building commenced, such an objective had become even less crucial to the endeavour's commercial success. When only a portage route linking the interior of the province to navigable water was projected, it made some sense to develop Hamilton as a deep-water port. But the emerging objective of providing a short and efficient link between American railroad systems could be better accomplished by the southern route, which struck west from Niagara Falls without having to descend the escarpment. The proposed Canadian trunk route from Toronto could be routed northward through Guelph and Kitchener (Berlin) to Port Stanley, across more leisurely gradients. That was precisely the route taken by the Grand Trunk, passing many miles north of the Dundas Valley. Only the commercial interests of the local shareholders and the Hamilton-dominated board dictated that the railway go anywhere close to the city and the Desjardins Canal.

Geological eras ago, following the end of the ice ages when the great inland Champlain Sea was receding, Burlington Heights presented a formidable north-south barrier preventing the waters in what is now known as Cootes Paradise from reaching present-day Hamilton Harbour. Seeking the path of least existence, the current slowly eroded a serpentine course around the northern limit of the heights. It was through this channel that the Desjardins Canal wound its way into the bay.

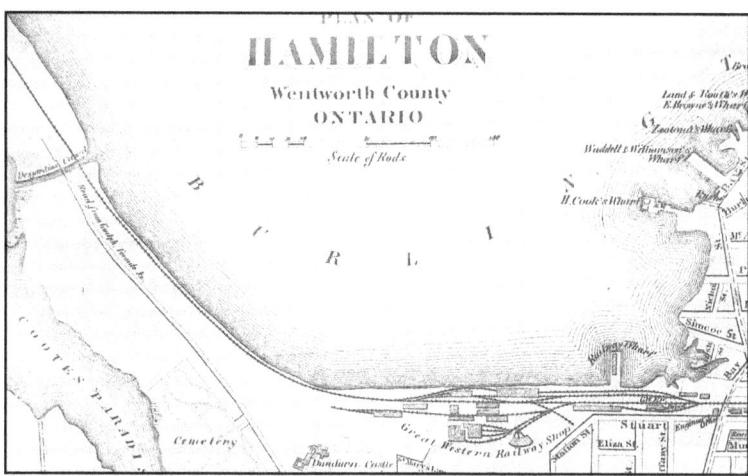

This map of early Hamilton in the 1870s shows the proximity of Dundurn Castle to the ill-fated bridge (far left), Cootes Paradise, the Great Western terminus, and Hamilton Cemetery, where many of the victims were buried.

AUTHOR'S COLLECTION.

Great Western Railway: Shovel Ready at Last

The original plan was to span the canal from the western flank, taking the railway through a smooth ninety-degree turn linking the heights and the start of the escarpment. The hope was that if sufficient height could be obtained for the bridge that it could be fixed — that is, that a movable draw span would not be necessary to provide clearance for the modest vessels capable of navigating the shallow draft canal.

Problems quickly began to mount. In order to find a solid foundation for the pilings that would support the trestle, the workers had to excavate a treacherous combination of gravel resting on a lethal layer of sand. The perilous technique was to dig a deep trench, then undermine the bank enough to dislodge the material above, and then to cart it away. In early February 1852 the inevitable occurred. Eleven workmen were clearing sand at the base of the bank when a length of about fifty feet suddenly subsided from about halfway up the almost perpendicular height. Ten of the workers (nine Irishmen and a German) were killed almost instantly — severely crushed and

The remains of the poorly constructed Great Western crossing of 12 Mile Creek, just outside Hamilton, are clearly visible from the replacement trestle. Just two months before the line opened in 1853 the whole structure began to slowly sink into the supported soil, revealing just how shoddy Zimmerman's makeshift construction techniques could be.

NIAGARA FALLS PUBLIC LIBRARY, 11952A.

suffocated. The eleventh worker, buried up to his head, was extricated by the foreman just before a second slide that would have sealed his fate.

The coroner's jury urged the adoption of alternative methods of excavation (ominously noting that the same technique had previously "proved fatal to some of the workmen"). What that alternative might be, the jury did not venture, but they absolved the contractors and overseers of all responsibility, on the grounds that they were only doing what they had done previously. The jury did take the opportunity to allude critically to "the circumstances of some of the workmen having been at work on this part of the road on the past Sabbath." While strongly condemning this, they again absolved the employers — noting that they forbade the practice. The local newspaper was even more anxious to show that the contractors were not culpable in this abuse of the Sabbath. In reporting the jury's findings, the *Spectator* commented: "The thing has been done without the consent of the contractors, and for the benefit of the men themselves, a few of whom did the work gratuitously, in order that the whole gang might not be idle on the following day." Given the state of labour-management relations at the time, and the well-deserved reputation for insubordination, hard drinking, and violence on the part of the navies at work on the railway, the characterization of voluntary philanthropy on the part of the labourers stretches credulity to the limit.

Labour was, in fact, a growing problem for the Great Western. The improved economic environment that made funds available for development created increasing demand for workmen. Wage rates began to rise until the common rate for railway construction on the line reached a staggering one dollar per day. Although Zimmerman held the construction contract, the actual labour was parcelled out to subcontractors who bid on individual sections, agreeing to terms based on the number of cubic yards of rock or soil removed and the number of board feet of timber supplied and installed. With labour and material prices sharply rising, these subcontractors regularly went bankrupt — walking away from the job. This necessitated re-letting the contracts at ever-higher rates. Workers sometimes arrived to find the old contractors had decamped without paying them and that new gangs hired by the new jobber were at work on the site.

In February 1851, the City of Hamilton petitioned the government to provide troops to control the 600 or so workers in the vicinity, noting that "many of the men engaged on the work have twice left their employment on demand for higher wages, and armed with bludgeons by threats of violence have drawn off and effectively prevented the peaceable and industrious labourers from earning a livelihood for themselves and their families." In Dundas, complaints were raised about gangs of thugs intimidating the workers and "brutally maltreating and abusing" the overseers.

Between Hamilton and London there were as many as two thousand men working on the railway. A great many of them were itinerant — such work offered no hope of permanent employment in a fixed location. They lived in crude camps, had limited social attachments, and frequently had little immediate purpose other than to struggle through until the next payday, when they could gorge themselves in an excess of drunken brawling. A large proportion were Irish immigrants, who, in addition to having endured the famine, the long sea journey to North America, and the devastating cholera of the 1830s, brought with them an ingrained antagonism toward authority and long-standing internal grudges. The pilfering and intimidation of these undisciplined bands did little to endear the railway to the local people.

Work on the canal bridge and approaches continued to be dogged by difficulties. In order not to disrupt boat traffic during the season, the two masonry abutments could not be constructed simultaneously. The cofferdam built to construct the eastern pier would have to be dismantled before construction on the western pier could commence. By January 1852 that cofferdam was supposed to have been filled in, but was flooded. The engineer, Roswell Benedict, ascribed the fault to "dilatory workmanship," which, he reported, left open the possibility that it would be destroyed by frost before the work could be secured.

About this time the canal company resurrected an earlier proposal to replace the planned trestle bridge with an embankment that would completely close off the canal exit and replace it with a fresh cut through the heights, significantly shortening and straightening the canal route. The railway originally declined this option because of the costs involved and because it would mean building a drawbridge rather than a fixed structure. With costs and delays spiralling, the engineer reassessed the proposal and the Great Western agreed to the scheme.

In recommending the new course of action, the engineer noted that the new structure would require only one-third the masonry as the initial plan — being only forty-four feet above the water, rather than the seventy-five feet required by the previous plan. The notion of a fixed structure had been abandoned, and it was argued that a drawbridge with a straight line of sight in both directions was preferable, for safety reason, to a draw span located on a ninety-degree curve. But the savings in time and cost made the difference. Since the new cut and bridge could be tackled without concern over impeding navigation, it could be aggressively pursued. Despite having already spent a considerable sum on foundations for the original structure, the substantially higher revised cost estimate meant that the new proposal would be some $35,000 cheaper than the old plan.

The dilatory workmanship the engineer Benedict had complained of was the responsibility of the subcontractors of Section 1, Messers Moore and McElroy. A few months after the change in plans, in March 1852, the railway declared their contract forfeited, in consequence of the failure to complete the work in proper time. New tenders were immediately issued and the contract re-let a few weeks later to the same Mr. Moore, this time without the participation of his partner McElroy.

Abetted by the squeaking of the aggrieved McElroy, at least one shareholder smelled something unsavoury in this outcome — especially since the price per yard of excavation apparently jumped by 50 per cent under the new deal. A good deal of rancour was vented at the next board meeting in June. One of the directors proffered the explanation that since the only practical manner of carrying off the excavated material entailed crossing Moore's property, his was the most advantageous proposal. Under questioning, the president professed no knowledge of the details of contracts, observing that such details were usually left in the hands of their engineer and solicitor.

All that might sound like the highly charged innuendo and impatient disdain that characterizes many a shareholder's meeting, even today. Yet the directors must have been better informed than they admitted. In fact, Benedict, the engineer, was a long-time friend of Samuel Zimmerman, and it was on Benedict's recommendation that he was appointed contractor for the central and eastern sections. That provided a most convenient situation, since the engineer exercised control over supply contracts, audited the construction results upon which payments were, based and controlled employment practices. When American investors initiated an inquiry into the desultory progress of construction, it was Benedict's own dereliction that came under scrutiny and he was forced to resign in November 1852.

He did not remain long in the shadows. In the spring of 1853 Benedict was appointed chief engineer of the Hamilton and Toronto Railway, then being constructed as a nominally independent, but fraternal company to the Great Western. Within a few months he moved to the London and Port Stanley, where he contracted the peripatetic Mr. Moore (this time a partner in the firm of Moore and Pierson) to construct the line. A few years later, Benedict and Ira Spaulding (another Zimmerman protégée) purchased a substantial portion of Zimmerman's surplus land at Niagara. In partnership with Pierson (of Moore and Pierson) he formed R.G. Benedict and Company, under which he pursued large-scale urban development in Niagara Falls. In the world of railway and business morality that prevailed in the 1850s, unravelling the intricacies of seemingly arm's length relationships was an exceedingly complex matter.

In his report of June 1852, while detailing the difficulties in the vicinity of the canal, Benedict confidently outlined the progress along the rest of the line. According to his account, the surveys had been comprehensively completed, much of the masonry for bridges and culverts had been placed on site, and contracts had been let for the railway shops in Hamilton. Benedict reported the work in such a forward state that grading could be complete as early as December 1852, with the completion of the superstructure in preparation for opening the line in August 1853.

Like their American counterparts, the British shareholders were suspicious of the real state of progress in Canada. While holding by far the greatest number of shares, they suspected that the Hamilton directors were managing affairs with a much greater concern for furthering local interests, collegial arrangements, and provincial politics than they were with ensuring a generous return on capital. Their response, at the urging of Peter Buchanan, the railway's London agent, was to appoint Charles John Brydges as managing director in the middle of 1852. Only twenty-six years old at the time, Brydges was a well-regarded assistant secretary with Britain's London and Southwestern Railway. His new position was deliberately created to ensure a greater degree of control over the Great Western by the British shareholders.

Undoubtedly dedicated to his employer's interests, Brydges brought an attitude that clashed with both the North American management style, and ultimately with the need of the British investors to exercise control. Even his mentor, Peter Buchanan, observed that he "require[d] a master over him and that party ought to be President with a couple of thousand a year and nothing else to do." Seemingly every operating decision on the Great Western required Brydges's approval — he was incapable of delegation. That not only undermined the confidence of his own officials, but led to a situation where only those who were content to avoid responsibility retained office. The result was a poorly managed railway in addition to a badly constructed line.

Great Western Railway: Shovel Ready at Last

After several unmet promises it was proposed that the railway would be opened in late 1854. The circumstances under which that came about illustrate both the authoritarian arrogance of Brydges and the abysmal disregard for human safety on the part of the Great Western.

On October 17, 1854, the chief engineer of the Great Western, John T. Clark, wrote an absolutely astounding letter to Managing Director C.J. Brydges. After noting that he understood that Brydges intended to "run a train of passenger cars over the eastern Division … on the first of November next," he went on: "And now for the purpose of relieving myself from all responsibility in a transaction I deem so imprudent and unwise, I desire to inform you in my official capacity, that I do not consider the grading or the superstructure, so far as it is laid down, in a safe condition to be used for public purposes."

Here was the one man charged with assessing the condition of the railway, absolutely and unequivocally stating that the line was unsafe. Brydges's response was, if possible, even more bizarre. First he castigated his engineer for prejudging the results of the official inspection, which Brydges argued could only be conducted after the contractor had declared the work complete (despite the obvious fact that by announcing his intention to open the line on a certain date, Brydges was quite clearly anticipating the outcome of that inspection). Then he baldly attempted to argue that his actions were driven by careful and balanced judgment. "It appears to me that a very grave responsibility rests upon any Board of Directors in neglecting to use a line of railway that is ready for use…. The public have a right to demand, that the earliest possible opportunity be afforded them of availing of a means of communication so essential as the Great Western Railway to the prosperity of the country at large." What arrant nonsense!

Brydges was not to be deterred. Not by argued reason and certainly not if that was advanced by an underling. He concluded his response to his engineer by writing: "I extremely regret that you should have so hastily pronounced an opinion upon a question which is not yet ripe for decision, and the more so, that the course you have taken will appear to place your views and my own at variance."

Poor Clark had no choice. Although that "train of passenger cars" had still not run by the third week of November, he addressed the board, remonstrating against the actions of the managing director's assumption of control over the engineering responsibilities and offering his resignation "in case of further palpable interference." Just two weeks later he had obtained a superior position as state engineer and surveyor for New York State, tendered his resignation, and received the approbation of the Board in which they regretted "that circumstances have compelled him to relinquish so

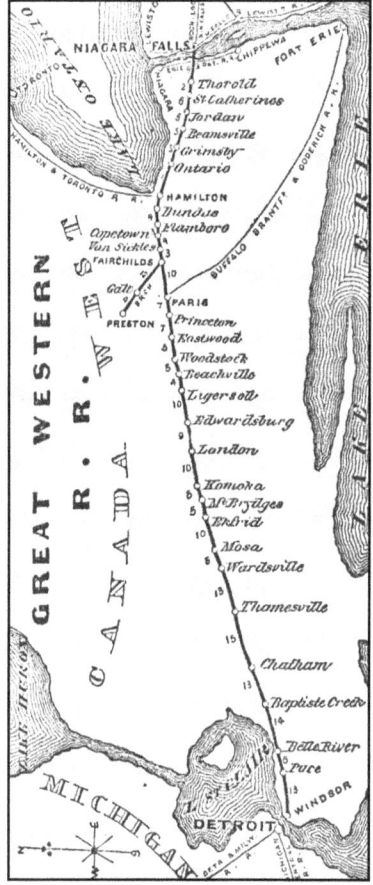

This 1856 company map shows the strategic importance of the Great Western as a shortcut, linking key U.S. lines and opening up the continental Midwest for trade with the eastern seaboard.

NIAGARA FALLS PUBLIC LIBRARY, D420465A.

soon the active duties of an office which you had filled with so much credit."

One year later, in conjunction with the government inquiry into the horrendous spate of fatal accidents that plagued that first year of operation, Brydges, determinedly unrepentant, continued to avow that his hand was forced. "I should have much preferred delaying the opening of any part of the line until the spring … that the public was most clamorous for it … that it would be hopeless to delay the opening after the track was actually completed … I conceived it better for both the public and the company that the line should be opened."

Modern railways are still built much as they were a century and a half ago. Metal-wheeled trains running on metal tracks are highly efficient, but quickly lose their effectiveness whenever the grade steepens even slightly. To obtain a level or gradually rising track, higher outcroppings are excavated as "cuttings" and lower levels are bridged or filled in as embankments (often using the rock and soil removed from the cuttings). The sides of the cuttings must be sloped. If the cutting sides are too vertical and too close to the actual track, debris loosened by erosion will collapse and block the line — possibly causing derailments. The tops of embankments must be wider than the tracks laid on them by a margin sufficient to prevent slippage from undermining the line, and they too must be sloped so as to avoid the sides from collapsing. Moreover, embankments must be perforated by culverts that allow for the free movement of surface water, or else they become dams that sooner or later will collapse under the inexorable force of built up pressure.

The metal tracks of most North American railroads are still spiked to wooden ties that are embedded in stone ballast. Anyone who has stood beside the line when a train rolls by will have noticed how sections of track are deflected slightly downward as the train rolls forward and then recoil when the pressure is removed. That "give" is crucial. Rigidly held in place on a rock-solid foundation, the rails would soon be fractured by the pounding of a heavy train. The combination of a wooden frame in a stone bed allows just enough spring to absorb some of that impact, without allowing the rails to bend so much that they might snap. Crushed-stone ballast serves several roles in that structure. The porous matrix allows for superior drainage — especially important in cold climates where a bed frozen solidly into one slab would provide as little "give" as concrete. The action of thousands of pieces of rock independently grinding against their neighbours allows for flexibility and resilience at the same time. Firmly packed ballast also serves to maintain the distance between ties, helping to hold the entire structure in place.

On the Great Western only a few miles of track were actually ballasted when the line was opened in the middle of winter. Three of the heaviest cuttings were little more than oversized channels, with steep sides and the grade anywhere from five to twelve feet above the intended permanent level. The railway's mechanical superintendent, William Bowman, was no less adamant than the former chief engineer that the line was in dangerous condition when opened. He testified during the Parliamentary inquiry that the cuttings were in "a most dangerous state, that there was no proper drainage, and the mud accumulated on the track in such a way as to make it hazardous to run trains." In some cuttings, he declared, the mud was three feet deep. Trains sometimes had to be divided because the slime was too heavy for the overpowered locomotive to draw out the entire train at one time.

Just two months before the line opened, the crossing over the Twelve Mile Creek at St. Catharines broke when the embankment slumped five and a half feet through the crude foundation on which it had been constructed, into soft clay. The base had been formed as a crude concrete pad, placed directly on the clay bed. On top of this wooden planks were laid, and then the massive twenty-five-foot high bank was simply piled up on top. The whole thing had taken a disgraceful two years to build and took only a few minutes to self-destruct. A 900-foot trestle had to be quickly cobbled together to temporarily carry the line around the breach.

When the line was opened, the engines and cars were "injured and wrenched and twisted and disabled by the roughness of the track." Bowman's locomotives were constantly out for repair. Springs and other parts were so strained that they frequently fractured unexpectedly. With only rudimentary repair facilities, Bowman was fighting a tough battle to keep trains running and had no confidence that he could keep them running safely.

Ready or not, C.J. Brydges had decided the Great Western must open. On November 10, 1853, the division between Hamilton and Niagara Falls was opened. Scarcely a month later, on December 12th, the first fatal accident occurred. Within a mile of Hamilton a westbound train collided with three cows that had been allowed to stray onto the track due to inadequate fencing. The engine, tender, baggage car, and three passenger cars were derailed. The fireman was badly crushed and died the following day. By that curious irony that seemed to dog the Great Western, the company's general manager saw for himself the consequences of operating an unsafe railway — C.J. Brydges himself was riding on the locomotive. And by yet another quirk of fate, the locomotive that took the first life was the Oxford — the same engine that took sixty more lives a little over three years later, when it dragged its train into the collapsing bridge over the Desjardins Canal.

In late December 1853 operations commenced on the stretch between Hamilton and London. Finally, in the middle of January 1854, the entire main line was put into service. For the promoters and the public served by the new facility it was an occasion for celebration.

On January 17, 1854, two twelve-car trains crawled along the entire route from Niagara Falls to Windsor. Four hundred guests from New York State and three hundred from the Hamilton-Toronto region were augmented by others who joined en route. Three hours later than the scheduled 2:00 p.m. arrival, the trains pulled into Windsor and the guests were ferried across the river to Detroit where they were treated to a magnificent dinner. Nearly 2,000 were seated in the commodious freight depot of the Michigan Central Railroad.

It was an extravagant display, punctuated by numerous toasts. A newspaper account commented: "… hardly one of the party had seen food or drink for twelve hours, and the way that the knives and forks were made to move, and the plates cleaned, and the champagne corks fly, must have been perfectly astonishing."

Two days later, it was Hamilton's turn to host a celebration. The *Hamilton Spectator* carried a glowing account of the festivities gushingly introduced with the following statement. "Hitherto not a single accident has occurred to mar this auspicious event, or to blend the slightest pain with the unbound pleasure everyone feels in the final accomplishment of one the most important works that has ever been made in the history of Canada, whether regarded in a moral, social, political, or, as a friend of ours would say, a metallic point of view." The relatives and friends of the unfortunate fireman killed barely a month earlier, and only a mile away, would be forgiven if they thought the writer's memory lapse just a little insensitive. But perhaps the comment reflected merely a happy surprise that the celebration excursion had been able to negotiate 200 miles of the Great Western's atrocious track without falling off the rails!

The train from Detroit was greeted with a twenty-one-gun salute from the artillery company. At 11:00 a.m. a procession, organized by the fire brigade, began its march along King Street. The parade's marshal was absent for some reason, so it was led by the Hamilton Artillery Company, headed by its captain, Alfred Booker Junior. Thus, Booker came to be at the forefront of the jubilation welcoming the same Great Western Railway that, a few years later, would claim his own father among its victims at the Desjardins Canal.

King Street was filled with uniforms as the militia, fire brigades, and bands marched along the street, accompanied by the city magistrates, aldermen, and the mayors of Hamilton and Rochester, New York, arm in arm. At the corner of James Street a triumphal arch had been erected, and there the parade halted and the Rochester Brass Band played the national anthem followed, at the request of a spectator, by a rousing rendition of "Yankee Doodle."

Great Western Railway: Shovel Ready at Last

At four in the afternoon a crowd of 600 firefighters from across the province (more than 200 from London alone) were hosted to a dinner in city hall by the local fire brigade. Catered by a James Street bakery and waited on by their own captains, the feast gave way to the usual round of toasts including one to "The Contractors on the Great Western Railway." That was responded to by the ubiquitous Mr. Moore.

Another dinner, hosted by the City of Hamilton, got underway later at the Mechanics' Institute. Most of the guests were from the United States and the delayed arrival of yet another train of dignitaries from Detroit, Chicago, and Milwaukee postponed commencement by a couple of hours. Catered by a local hotel, it was clearly a lavish event. In fact, in preparation a special messenger had been dispatched to Chicago with instructions to "purchase, regardless of expense, anything in the shape of game to be procured from the far west."

At the time, North America's railways were only on the cusp of filling a previously unrecognized need. The lavish and exotic menus of these celebratory dinners could not have been possible without the railroads' abilities to rush provisions to the table while still fresh and appealing. While smaller communities had more immediate access to local produce, in the 1850s the only way to enjoy fresh milk in larger cities, like New York, was to send a servant into the country to collect it — a significant excursion before railways. Within a decade or so, farming operations were being concentrated within reach of the rails and the catchment area was expanding exponentially. By the 1860s it was possible to buy fresh tomatoes, citrus fruits, and other previously unattainable produce in any major North American centre, every day of the year. By the standards of the day, the magnificent banquets mounted to promote the arrival of the Great Western must have been by any stretch both extraordinarily unique and highly memorable.

Of the Hamilton dinner, the *Spectator* wryly observed: "The wines, we feared, tempted many of our Michigan friends, who had taken advantage of the occasion to satisfy themselves of the progress which the Canadians were making toward the Maine Liquor Law, now working so satisfactorily in their own State." That laconic reference was to an early prohibition initiative, banning the sale of alcohol except for "medicinal, mechanical or manufacturing purposes." First introduced in Maine in 1851, the measure spread quickly across many of the northern states and had been implemented in Michigan the previous year, only to be struck down by the courts. Although there were early Canadian proponents, no similar measures were adopted until after Confederation, and those proved less prohibitionist and more concerned with the taxation and regulation of liquor sales, forming the basis of today's widespread government monopoly in the liquor trade. Despite some heavyweight champions, the U.S. legislation was broadly unpopular and difficult to enforce, even in Maine. The Portland Rum Riots of 1855 erupted when that city's Irish immigrant population, who viewed the act as racially biased, interrupted a court hearing. In the ensuing tumult one person was killed and a number injured by government troops. The following year the Maine legislation was withdrawn.

Clearly, the *Spectator*'s reporter was unimpressed by any contributions the Michigan law had made toward general sobriety, and must have been amused by the alacrity with which the visitors took full advantage of the Great Western's open hospitality.

The toasts were fulsome. None more so than the resounding praise directed toward Sir Allan MacNab. Sir Allan was absent from all this revelry, but clearly not forgotten. During the afternoon a deputation of the Artillery had paid an impromptu visit to Dundurn Castle, where gouty Sir Allan was confined to bed. There they announced that if the health of the "Father of the Railway" would permit, they would like to honour him with a royal salute. Highly gratified, Sir Allan accepted their offer and later in the evening the entire company, accompanied by "a large concourse of citizens," arrived on the castle grounds and fired a twenty-one-gun salute. Rising from his sickbed, ruddy-faced Sir Allan delivered a brief message of thanks from his bedroom window. After three mighty cheers the assemblage trooped back to the city.

Great Western Railway: Shovel Ready at Last

The jubilation was fully warranted. The impact of early railways on widely separated populations is without modern parallel. They did not merely speed up transportation, they made possible the shipment of goods that were previously too bulky, too fragile, or too perishable to travel great distances. Mail that had taken several days to reach communities along the line could be delivered in a matter of hours. Newspapers could inform and persuade broader audiences in faster time. People could shuttle in unheard of comfort between cities and towns. The whole pace of commerce was accelerated. The Great Western delivered opportunity and prosperity for miles around every town along its route. For its promoters it was a resounding success. But, while its economic contributions were warmly applauded, the operations of the line were so abysmally deficient as to cast a pall over the entire endeavour.

During the first few months of operation there was a spate of accidents that suggest the railway staff were ill disciplined and unsuited for the responsibilities of running a railroad. Notwithstanding a company regulation that provided for summary dismissal in the case of intoxication, drinking was evidently a significant problem. In March, near Chatham, a handcar carrying four drunken employees collided with a train, killing one and severely injuring two others. Several instances were recorded of drunks lying on the track being run over and killed.

Some of these accidents, while not resulting in great loss of life, were more ominous. At the end of February "Oxford" again featured in an accident — this time just to the west of Hamilton, not far beyond the Desjardins bridge. A westbound train was ordered out of Hamilton without proper clearance and collided with the Oxford on the Dundas trestle. Earlier in the month a freight train and a gravel train collided within a mile or two of the same spot. That April a large stone was dislodged from the steep side of a cutting near Niagara Falls, causing considerable damage to a train that ran into it.

Since all of the victims had so far been employees or trespassers, the Great Western was able to report, after six months of operation, that it had achieved commercial success without losing the life of a single passenger. In the summer months, perhaps as speeds began to pick up, the death toll began to cause greater consternation. In June, six passengers were killed in an incident that clearly demonstrated the cavalier attitude of the company toward operating methods and the care of their passengers. This accident was what first aroused widespread alarm and ultimately triggered an official inquiry into the abysmal safety record of the company.

A huge wave of European immigration was opening up the American west. For the railroads this was lucrative. The Great Western, and other lines, employed agents to funnel passengers onto their line. A party of Norwegians had contracted with such an agent in Quebec for their transport through to Chicago. In early June 1854 the group was herded into a freight car attached to a westbound train. Eventually this train reached the town of Chatham, where an Irishman similarly confined to the same freight car complained of being carried beyond his stop, London. With callous disregard for the other occupants, the stationmaster blithely ordered the car attached to the next eastbound train. The confused Norwegians found themselves travelling back over the route they had recently passed.

Some miles west of London, at Lobo, the train approached a high embankment. Like so much of the company's infrastructure, it was incomplete. There were no fences on either of the approaches and the top of the embankment was scarcely wider than the track it supported. Two cows had wandered onto the structure — with no possibility of escaping the oncoming train. All the evidence suggests that although the cows must have been visible for a considerable distance, the engineer, rather than making any attempt to stop, adopted the expedient of attempting to drive them off the line.

Understandably, with so little of the line fenced, there was considerable friction between the company and farmers. The latter complained of the many animals lost, while there were veiled suggestions, by some, that some animals were herded onto the line so that compensation could be claimed when they were killed. A number of drivers probably made no effort to avoid cattle on the line. Many believed that if the animals were not deflected completely the superior weight of the engine made it unlikely that it would be derailed — even if the cars they were hauling would be. That is, indeed, what happened at Lobo.

The engine and tender, the Reindeer, stayed on the track. The following first- and second-class cars, along with the freight car containing the immigrants, were derailed. The first simply teetered on the top of the embankment; the second landed on its side halfway down. The freight car somersaulted to land upside down at the foot of the slope, broken into a hundred pieces. Five Norwegians and an American were killed. Fourteen other passengers were injured.

At the Coroner's Inquest the railway, through its spokesperson C.J. Brydges, defended the practice of transporting immigrants in freight cars (despite collecting fares based on second-class travel). With unctuous hypocrisy, Brydges claimed that immigrants preferred to travel in freight cars since they were able to stay close to their belongings, enabling them to spread out bedding and consume their own food. If this weren't fatuous enough, Brydges went on to argue that the immigrants would have been no safer travelling in a second class car since: "The seats in the second class cars were very cumbersome, and had many nails and sharp points; in this case they were all torn up, and together with the passengers [had fallen] to the further end of the car." He argued that the poorly secured seats and exposed nails would have been as likely to cause damage to persons as the loose baggage. One can only imagine what degree of comfort that must have provided other patrons of the company's second-class cars.

Several more incidents occurred over the next few months. Later in June a tracklayer removed a rail half an hour before an express was due, and failed to put any warning flags in place at all. Two passengers were killed.

In July 1854 seven immigrants were killed when a train collided with two horses on a level crossing. C.J. Brydges defended the outcome by pointing out that since it was night the incident could not have been avoided. The Commission of Inquiry felt otherwise. They believed the night to have been clear and the line of sight uninterrupted. They harboured a strong suspicion that Great Western drivers continued to believe that the most expeditious means of handling livestock on the track was to drive them off with speed and momentum.

The commission unearthed several incidents that showed the almost unimaginable degree of heartlessness prevailing throughout the management of the railway. Even Charles Dickens might have found it hard to credit.

In the course of conducting its investigation into the collision with the horses the inquiry commissioners visited Thorold, where the incident occurred. To their horror they were regaled with details of an event that had happened only the day prior to their arrival. On December 7th, repairs were still underway on the massive slippage at St. Catharines that had occurred before the railway opened. The temporary trestle over the Twelve Mile Creek was still in place. On that day a twelve-year-old boy, John Donally, was employed providing water to the workers at the western end of the structure. He left his home at the eastern end with a bucket of water and, it being a cold day, had the earflaps on his cap tied down in order to keep warm. He obviously did not hear an approaching train as it rounded a steep curve, and whether he saw the lad or not, the engine driver certainly did not blow his whistle. The boy was hit, badly injured in his leg and elsewhere, and thrown down the embankment where he was found half-frozen three-quarters of an hour later. The commissioners concluded that the engineer had displayed an absolutely callous degree of inhumanity — neither stopping to render assistance nor alerting the workers on the other side of the incident. The commissioners rather reluctantly accepted the engineer's claim that he did not see the boy nor realize that he had hit him. In that event they could only characterize his ignorance as a reflection of a gross negligence of duty, since under such circumstances especially he should have been keeping a sharp lookout.

Around this time there was a serious outbreak of cholera, and immigrants crammed into close proximity onboard ships were seriously affected. Medical examinations were conducted at point of first landing, but a great many cases went undetected. There can be no doubt that the party of Norwegian immigrants who boarded a Great Western train in Hamilton in early July were already infected, but they could not have realized how hellish a journey they were about to embark upon. Within minutes of starting the trip they experienced their first delay. The notorious Desjardins embankment was, yet again, out of commission. The footings had slipped and a serious collapse occurred that made it necessary to ferry passengers and freight around the breach. On the other side the immigrants were herded into freight cars and sent on their way. In the vicinity of Chatham, at Baptiste Creek, the excruciating heat had buckled the rail resulting in the derailment of a gravel train. With an eastbound and a westbound train trapped on either side of the obstacle the solution was obvious — the passengers of each were exchanged and their trains reversed. But there were no second-class cars, so the immigrant cars were simply run onto a siding and essentially abandoned.

In the stifling heat, with little or no command of English, the now-sickly immigrants were forced to forage for themselves in the neighbourhood, with only swamp water to quench their thirst. When the obstruction was cleared the cars were pulled the remaining thirty-two miles into Windsor, some thirty hours later. By then it was quite clear that cholera was rampant. Four died that day and over the ensuing two or three weeks a great many more. The final tally may have been as high as seventy, and included a number of local residents as well as the immigrants. Being crammed as many as forty to fifty per freight car in the stifling heat certainly did nothing to ease the suffering and must have accelerated the spread of the disease. The Commission of Inquiry satisfied itself that the inexcusable insensitivity of the railway directly contributed to the death toll.

Railway accidents sometimes make fascinating study since they demonstrate the extreme difficulty of anticipating every eventuality and the challenge of providing a safeguard for every hazard. The accident at the Desjardins Canal is a case in point. Even today it could not be guaranteed that a similar axle failure might not trigger a set of events that could end with equal calamity. Indeed, a 1998 accident involving a German ICE train at Eschede that resulted in the deaths of a hundred people has remarkable similarities.

There can be no mitigating claims of ill fortune about the accident that occurred on October 16, 1854, at Baptiste Creek; there are no lessons to be learned, no safeguards that could be devised and installed. That is because the accident that took the lives of fifty-two people was the result of an astonishing degree of pig-headed ignorance and arrogance.

The story is simply told. The vast amount of ballasting so urgently needed on the Great Western had been placed in the hands of independent contractors. George Harris operated a gravel pit at Baptiste Creek, from which he delivered ballast to nearby sections of the line. The Great Western provided the trains used in the operations as well as the train personnel, but the contractor met their payroll. Strict rules were in place that the gravel train should remain off the main line until scheduled trains had passed.

That employees, so remote from management supervision, might develop a closer sympathy for the contractor who paid them than for the railway that appointed them is perhaps not surprising. Certainly that appears to have been the case with the conductor of the ballast train, T.D. Twitchell. Contrary to what many commonly believe, the engineer is not in charge of a train, the conductor is. The conductor orders the train to proceed and he ensures that all the necessary steps are taken to guard against adverse traffic.

Before the days of telegraph there was no way of knowing the status of trains that had fallen behind the timetable. The westbound mail express was scheduled to pass Baptiste Creek just after 10:00 p.m. each evening. Until this train had passed, the ballast train was under orders to remain sidetracked. This, of course, was not in the contractors' interest, and since the express could be notoriously late.

Conductor Twitchell had occasionally been tempted to make a quick trip out in contravention of the rules — sometimes as many as four times in one night. This was nothing less than a game of Russian roulette, played with bullets the size of railway trains.

So blatantly foolhardy were these forays onto the mainline that the locomotive engineer, John Kettlewell, had quite properly complained to the engineering department. This brought the following explicit injunction to Twitchell from Thomas Gregory, Resident Engineer of the Western Division:

> I have to request that you do not run on Express time, but be off the Main Track twenty minutes before it is due, and remain till it has passed. Any transgression of this rule will be reported to me, and will call for a demand on my part for your dismissal. The whole weight and responsibility of any accident that may happen from a transgress of this will fall upon your shoulders.

That missive was dated October 14, 1854. Around five o'clock in the morning of October 27th the ballast train once again ventured onto the main line. This time the chamber was full and the game of roulette ended in disaster. No steps were taken to post a watchman or place a warning signal to protect the train.

The Mail Express had been having a tough run. It left Niagara Falls on schedule at 2:00 p.m. on the 26th. At St. George, near Brantford, it was delayed more than an hour by a derailed gravel train and then by slow traffic. It reached London almost two hours late, and only a couple of miles beyond that station the engine broke down. A new engine was dispatched — the very same Reindeer that was involved in the Lobo crash.

In the swampy vicinity of Baptiste Creek, and in the foggy darkness of an October morning at 5:10 a.m., the express encountered the cars of the loaded ballast train as they were being propelled forward by engineer Kettlewell. Although the express was only proceeding at a rate of about twenty-five miles an hour, the heavy ballast train offered less resilience than a stone wall. The mail-train engine veered to one side and passenger cars piled up against the obstruction.

The location was remote, with only one farmhouse within a mile. It took hours before help could arrive and little equipment was available. Officially fifty-two lives were lost — a horrendous toll, and the very worst that had been experienced at that time anywhere in Canada or the United States.

The coroner's jury found Twitchell and Kettlewell guilty of manslaughter and charges were laid. In the case of the engineer proceedings seem rather unfair, since the conductor was in charge of the train and Kettlewell had clearly taken fully justified steps to alert authorities to Twitchell's unauthorized forays. The jury did, however, qualify his as having the lower culpability.

There were absolutely no mitigating circumstances to in any way minimize the recklessness that resulted in the Baptiste Creek tragedy. The conductor, in defiance of the most basic prudence and in complete disobedience of the most explicit instruction to obey the rules, took an unassailably foolish risk. No one took any of the most basic steps to protect the train — by placing warning signals or posting a watchman. And management, having been alerted to a dangerous practice, took insufficient steps to prevent its recurrence. No amount of safety measures can ever truly guard against complete disregard of the rules.

The accident did have one immediate effect. It was the straw that broke the camel's back. The simmering concern over the company's shocking safety record and its arrogant contempt of human life led Governor General Lord Elgin to appoint William F. Coffin and M.C. Cameron to report to the Legislative Assembly on "A series of Accidents and Detentions on the Great Western Railway." That such an unusual investigation should be established in an era of capital supremacy and *caveat emptor* is an astonishing testament to just how widespread public antipathy toward the dilatory and callous practices of the Great Western had become.

Great Western Railway: Shovel Ready at Last

The inquiry was wide-ranging and the report extensive. The findings comprehensively detailed the failings of the company to complete the basic engineering responsibilities essential to safe operations before opening the line, such as stabilizing structures, establishing appropriate grades and construction gauges, providing fencing, and installing adequate warning devices. To prevent future recurrences, the commissioners recommended the establishment of a public railway inspectorate with powers to require compliance with safety standards before granting authority to open new lines.

Their report was highly critical of the decision to open the railway in an unfinished state. While politically circumspect in their criticism of the company itself, the commissioners were quicker in their condemnation of the management and employees. In censuring the role C.J. Brydges played in pressing the unfinished line into use, they remarked:

> From information received from C.J. Brydges, Esq., the Managing Director of the Great Western Railway Company, it appears that the system of management in force in the Great Western Railway Company is unknown to those familiar with the administration of Railroads in America. The whole machinery of a complicated enterprise is not only superintended or directed, but is actually and practically worked out, or attempted to be worked out by one man. The Managing Director is not only the head but the hand to which every important duty is confided. That officer, whose natural talents, industry and zeal are universally admitted, has assumed or has had imposed on him more duties than one man can possible accomplish.

While cast in deliberately guarded language, that condemnation was a severe damnation of Brydges arrogance and dictatorial management style. His "natural talents, industry and zeal" — to say nothing of his profitable administration — more than offset his shortcomings in the eyes of his corporate masters. Brydges maintained his position until resigning in 1862 to take over as general manager of the even larger operations of the Grand Trunk Railway.

CHAPTER EIGHT

BRIDGES AND BRYDGES

The Suspension Bridge and Brydges the Managing Director of the G.W.R.R.
— TOAST PROPOSED BY THE REPRESENTATIVE OF ALBANY, N.Y.,
AT THE HAMILTON CELEBRATIONS

That toast was a transparently contrived and clumsily delivered effort, but it proclaimed a truth — it took both people and structures to make the Great Western. Of all those structures, none were more critical than the bridges, and of those there were many examples from lowly culverts spanning muddy rivulets to one of the most imposing engineering achievements of the era, the Suspension Bridge over the Niagara River.

Strictly speaking the Suspension Bridge was not a Great Western structure. The railway did not own it, but it was built to meet the needs of the railway and the Great Western leased the upper deck, over which it shuttled its traffic between the United States and Canada. Without this bridge, the Great Western had no way of fulfilling its ambition of providing a shortcut for American traffic to and from the Midwest.

END OF THE LINE

In 1848 a carriage suspension bridge had been strung across the Niagara Gorge. This was no mean feat. Since ferrying a cable across the river was impossible, the designer hit upon the notion of offering a $5 reward to the first person to launch a kite from one side to the other. From this fragile line successively stronger chords were strung, until a 230-metre bridge could be built. So phenomenally successful was this enterprise that it was soon earning an 8 percent return per month.

That was attraction enough to interest the likes of Samuel Zimmerman (who had a hand in its construction). With Zimmerman as contractor, along with the other proponents of the railway as investor, the idea of an international railway bridge was born. The designer was John Roebling, who was later to become famous for his most noteworthy creation, the mighty Brooklyn Bridge in New York.

This contemporary postcard captures the spirit of the amazing 1855 Suspension Bridge. It was truly a construction marvel that predated New York's more famous Brooklyn Bridge and caused engineers to stand in awe of the audacity of its design. Built within view of the famous falls, crossing an international boundary, and forming a vital link in both countries westward expansion, it was a wonder of its day.

PUBLIC DOMAIN.

When the Suspension Bridge was opened for traffic in March 1855 it was the world's longest railway bridge. Of the path-breaking plan to employ a suspension span rather than a rigid form to support the railway, Robert Stephenson, the globe-trotting civil and mechanical engineer, whose father, George, built the first steam railways, observed: "If your bridge succeeds then mine have been magnificent failures."

The bridge was audacious in many ways. Since it was intended to carry other traffic as well as trains, Roebling built a double-decked design. Through the covered interior carriages, carts, cattle, and pedestrians crossed. On the upper deck trains rolled on four rails laid to accommodate three different gauges. The bridge offered an incomparably spectacular view of the Horseshoe Falls, and when Zimmerman expanded his financial empire by opening the Zimmerman Bank a few months after the inauguration of the bridge, he selected an engraving of that view to grace his banknotes.

Although suspension never became a popular principle for the designers of railway bridges, this truly magnificent structure lasted forty years before being replaced with a more modern structure. In fact, even the most humble spans built in the 1850s would become notable if they endured for forty years — the great majority crumbled in a much shorter time and a good many collapsed under the weight of the traffic they were intended to service.

Relatively few of the smaller bridges in the early days of North American railroading were engineered — they were constructed. They were built by men typically experienced only with pedestrian or cart traffic, and to the extent they were designed at all they were planned according to what "looked" solid. If they exhibited signs of insufficiency they were retrofitted with braces and additional stabilizers wherever weaknesses seemed in evidence.

Roads could often cross seasonal or shallow watersheds by means of fords or ferries, and where bridges were essential they could often be built only a few feet above the water. As a result, there was hardly any experience with building the high-level bridges required to keep railway grades manageable — even less with those that would have to withstand the heavy weights and vibrations a train could generate. Moreover, the many bridges demanded by the rapid expansion of the railroad had to be built economically.

Little wonder then that the proliferation of timber-built railway bridges had design lives of considerably less than a decade — and that a frightening proportion had even that short expectancy cut short by spring floods, heaving frost, or simply the passage of a train.

Railway travel, even in its infancy, could be readily understood by the travelling public. They might be in awe of the mystical workings of the engine, but they could usually tell when a train was travelling at too rapid a pace. They could tell when the cars

A brochure designed for tourists captures the romantic lure of Niagara Falls, the engineering achievement of the Suspension Bridge, and the practical advantages of travelling the route.

PUBLIC DOMAIN.

were rolling dangerously or snatching too sharply. They could obviously understand the risks posed by obstructions on the track, or worse still an opposing train improperly routed onto the track their train was travelling. But bridges were something of a mystery for many, and many were extremely uncomfortable being suspended many feet above deep water, relying on the builder's skill. That discomfort was heightened by the knowledge that faith had so often proved unjustified.

Even as late as 1879, one author, Charles Francis Adams, argued that while the cause and consequences of many accidents could be recognized, "It is by no means always so in the case of accidents on bridges. With these the cause of the disaster is apt to be so scientific in its nature that it cannot even be described, except through the

So advanced was the bridge that while trains ran over the top deck, a second level allowed horse-drawn carriages, livestock, and pedestrians to travel below. Note its generous dimensions, effectively making a second "covered bridge" spanning the 825-foot width of the Niagara Gorge.

NIAGARA FALLS PUBLIC LIBRARY, D422285.

use of engineering terms which to the mass of readers are absolutely incomprehensible. The simplest of railroad bridges is an inexplicable mystery to at least ninety-nine persons out of each hundred."

Railroad wrecks have had a prominent place in history. Those involving bridges, where the death tolls were nearly always magnified, were frequently elevated to the status of folklore. The very thought of being simultaneously torn by jagged splinters as well as trapped in frigid waters must have seemed a most awful form of double jeopardy.

Probably the most "celebrated" wrecks in American railroad history occurred at Angola, New York, and at Ashtabula, Ohio. Both happened on Cornelius Vanderbilt's Lake Shore Road, both occurred around Christmas, and both involved bridges.

Quickly tagged the "Angola Horror" by the press, the first had some similarities to the Desjardins disaster, although it occurred ten years later. A week before Christmas Day in 1867, the eastbound Lake Shore Express was approaching the bridge over Three Sisters Creek with a slightly deformed axle on the rear truck of the rear car. The bent axle struck a frog in the track (part of the switch), derailed, and was dashed against the bridge abutment. The preceding car also broke free and dropped over the side of the bridge. Hot coals from the stove ignited the rubble and forty-two passengers died — many of them burned alive.

The second of these two accidents occurred on December 29, 1876. Just as the leading locomotive of the westbound Pacific Express reached the far end of the Ashtabula Bridge the engineer heard a crack and felt the structure begin to sag. Can an engineer ever have had so close a brush with death? In an instant he yanked open the throttle. His locomotive surged, the coupling between it and the tender parted, and he reached safety. The rest of his train was not so lucky. The front part of it plunged with the collapsing bridge, while subsequent cars shot into the void and crashed into a pile on the floor of the ravine, sixty-nine feet below.

Once again fire ensued and at least eighty people perished. There was, in fact, some doubt about the number of casualties. Many of the townspeople, including the mayor, were railroad employees. In the confusion, authorities apparently made no effort to douse the flames, despite the availability of pumps, hoses, and a ready supply of water in the shallow creek, which ran through the ravine. Some saw that as connivance with the railway to obscure the true death toll. Some revisionists have placed it as high as 150 out of a possible 200 onboard.

However many it killed directly, it most likely claimed two or three more lives after the fact. The ensuing enquiry found the design and maintenance of the iron Howe truss bridge defective. Charles Collins, the railway's chief engineer and the man responsible for overseeing repairs, immediately took his own life.

The designer disavowed responsibility, claiming that the railroad's president, Amasa Stone, had provided explicit specifications for the structure. In fact, he claimed, his remonstrations against the design's shortcomings resulted in his being fired just after the completion of the span. The public animosity raised against Stone was the cause, according to some, of his suicide some five years later.

Since Cornelius Vanderbilt himself died just four days after the accident, there are those who assert that it hastened his demise. Those who knew more of the Commodore's thick-skinned feistiness might have been reluctant to endorse that theory!

Sometimes railway bridge incidents gained notoriety not for the size of casualty list, but for the prominence of those involved, even if they were among the survivors. One such incident occurred on June 29, 1882, when a train carrying wealthy New Jersey residents on their way to their New York offices derailed on a wooden trestle. The last five cars toppled into the tidal marsh that formed the banks of Parkers Creek.

Although the incident was serious enough — five people lost their lives in the shallow water — a lot of attention was drawn to the fate of Long Branch, New Jersey's most famous resident of the time.

Like so many fellow travellers, former U.S. president, and then-prominent Manhattan broker, Ulysses S. Grant was obliged to crawl from the side of his disabled car and wallow his way to safety.

Misfortune touched the life of a man far more identified with his era than even the president of the United States. Charles Dickens, chronicler of his times, was a man so quintessentially Victorian as to seem today more Victorian than her imperial majesty herself. On June 9, 1865, the South Eastern Railway's Folkestone Boat Express was headed toward that seaside town on England's southeast coast. Before the greater development of the port the timing of cross-channel ferries was governed by the state of the tide. As a consequence, the train, known colloquially as the "Tidal," ran on an irregular schedule to accommodate the sailings.

On this particular day, work was underway at Staplehurst, Kent, to replace the timber baulks that supported the rails and were placed across the cast-iron girders of a bridge spanning a salt marsh just ten feet below it. The railway staff engaged in this operation had mislaid the operating timetable and, under the mistaken belief that the light Sunday traffic allowed them far more time than they really had, disgracefully inadequate precautions were taken.

Although the driver of the express whistled for brakes immediately when he encountered the danger signal, there was woefully insufficient distance to bring the train up. The engine and leading van managed to cross the gap created by the failure of the work gang to replace two sections of rail, but the strain was too great, causing one of the cast iron girders to collapse. Five of the following carriages were turned into splintered wreckage in the muddy streambed. Ten passengers perished and a further forty-nine others were injured.

Dickens, seated in the rear of the train, was not apparently injured. He was, at the time, engaged in reviewing the manuscript of *Our Mutual Friend*. In a postscript to that book he described the accident and how, when he had rendered whatever assistance he could to other victims, he returned to his carriage to rescue the manuscript "much soiled, but otherwise unhurt."

While superficially unscathed, the author was not unaffected. He subsequently complained: "I am curiously weak, weak as if I were recovering from a long illness. I begin to feel it more in my head. I sleep well and eat well; but I write half a dozen words and turn faint and sick." Dickens clearly related these developments to the accident itself. He was reluctant to resume train travel, but when he did, he complained of "A perfect conviction against the senses, that the carriage is down on one side (and generally that is the left, and not the side on which the carriage in the accident really went over) comes upon me with anything like speed, and is increasingly distressing."

Dickens's conduct in the immediate aftermath was highly praised. The literary icon of his age did his best to provide comfort to the dying and injured — plying them with brandy from his personal flask and water he transported in his hat. Victorian readers were, however, not provided all the details of his activities that day. He was accompanied in the carriage by his mistress, Ellen Ternan, with whom he was returning from a holiday in Paris. With consummate discretion, Dickens wrote to railway officials a little later enquiring about a gold watch and chains lost in the confusion by "a lady who was in the carriage with me." He had "promised the lady to make her loss known at headquarters, in case these trinkets should be found." More explicit details neither the railway officials nor the public at large were entitled to!

Dickens continued to be affected up to his death, five years to the day after the accident. Whether his end was accelerated by the negligence of the South Eastern Railway's work gang is open to question, but in light of his resultant loss of concentration, as one writer has suggested, it seems certain to have deprived English literature of Dickens solution to the unfinished *Mystery of Edwin Drood*.

Of all the Victorian railway bridge disasters in Britain — and indeed around the world — undoubtedly the greatest was the 1879 collapse of the bridge over the Tay Estuary in Scotland. The tale is replete with high drama: triumphant engineering turned into public humiliation, wild, stormy Scottish winter weather, desperate and dangerous attempts at rescue, and, ultimately, the numbing realization that all seventy-five souls on board had been lost. So deeply did it scar the British psyche that one hundred years after the event, *The Times of London* dedicated a whole page to revisiting the horror.

The east coast route from the Scottish south to Aberdeen is sliced by the two great tidal estuaries of the Forth and the Tay. Travellers by the North British Railway in the 1870s were forced to abandon their snug railway carriages and embark on steam ferries across the gaps. The harsh Scottish weather often made these voyages perilous and, at times, impossible. To address this traffic interruption, the NBR commissioned Thomas Bouch to design and construct bridges across the gaps.

Construction started first on the more northern crossing of the Tay. To the lay eye, the design did not instill confidence. Cast-iron pillars mounted on stone piers were placed across the river, topped by iron box trestles over which the trains passed. In order to provide sufficient clearance for the tall-masted naval and commercial vessels of the day, the girders above the shipping channel were raised on the highest piers and the trains travelled through these "high girders," rather than on top of them. There were problems from the beginning. The cast-iron piers were a change from the original plan that had called for all-masonry supports.

As it became clear that the foundations under the river were less firm than believed, lighter cast-iron columns were substituted. Subsequent to the accident it was determined that the calculation of the maximum wind resistance that the structure would encounter was exceptionally naive — even though it was provided by no less august a being than the "Astronomer Royal."

There was an even more insidious factor at play. Cast iron is an inherently dangerous construction material — imperfections introduced during the difficult process of casting can remain hidden beneath the surface, only to be exposed as critical weaknesses under load. The material used in the construction of the Tay Bridge had more sinister flaws than these intrinsic defects — among other dilatory practices, it was the habit of the onsite foundry workers to disguise any visible blemishes in the casting by filling them with a substance known as Beaumont egg, a mixture of iron filings and beeswax that could be buffed to the colour of iron.

With all its hidden faults, the bridge was put into service on June 1, 1878. For its designer and the railway it was an unmitigated triumph. The two-mile-long structure, which at its highest point stood eighty-eight feet above high tide, represented the very summit of Victorian knowhow and daring. Its designer had begun work on the second crossing, of the Firth of Forth, and although he was not a part of the engineering establishment his efforts were about to be rewarded with the most prized recognition any Victorian could aspire to, a knighthood. The following summer, Her Majesty, a reluctant although practical patron of the railways, deigned to cross the bridge on her way south from her Scottish estate at Balmoral. Shortly afterward, Thomas Bouch became Sir Thomas. How quickly was his esteem to be shattered!

The weather on December 28, 1879, was foul. The Firth was no stranger to strong winds and vile conditions, but the winds driving heavy rain up the channel that night were extreme, even for that location. Gust after gust battered the St. Fort station on the south side of the span and toppled chimney tops in Dundee at the north end.

As the train approached the bridge around seven o'clock that night, the passengers had already endured the stormy ferry crossing of the Firth of Forth on their way north from Edinburgh. In spite of the tempest outside they must have heaved a sigh of satisfaction that they could enjoy the journey into Dundee in the comparative luxury of their railway carriage.

As the train passed the St. Fort signal box and moved onto the bridge, the signalmen noticed sparks shooting from the wheels of the last carriage. These were later determined to be the result of the furious wind pushing the train against the leeward rail. The gusts were sufficiently strong, in fact, that when the entire complement had entered the high girders the resistance offered by the girders and train together proved simply too much. The high spans containing the train collapsed into the Firth. On shore and at anchor on the water, a few people actually witnessed the disaster, but so dark was the night and the rain was so fierce that it was some time before the reality could be verified.

In all some seventy-five persons lost their lives, although only forty-six bodies were recovered. A commission of enquiry determined that the bridge suffered from inadequate design, defective material, and insufficient maintenance. They held Sir Thomas Bouch chiefly to blame. Work on the Firth of Forth Bridge was immediately suspended and the structure completely redesigned, as one of the most massive of Victorian structures. Sir Thomas was humiliated. The engineering elite who had reluctantly adopted him when he was flush with success was delighted to disown him again. Dispirited and nervous, he died only ten months later.

Despite the heavy toll of life, there is something heroic about the Tay Bridge disaster. It was, after all, the end result of an effort to push the boundaries of technology — a daring and visionary attempt to tame geography. In contrast to the two-mile chord stretched across the Tay, the hundred-foot span over the Desjardins Canal in distant Canada West may seem inconsequential. But it took nearly as many lives, had an even more immediate impact on its community, raises as many questions about bridge design and construction, and is every bit as gripping a tale of human interest as the vastly more famous Scottish incident.

In early May 1853 an American bridge wreck occurred that had a strange significance for the Desjardins Canal catastrophe. A negligent engineer ignored the absence of a signal that would have indicated that a drawbridge ahead of him was safe for passage. His New Haven Railroad locomotive plunged into the open draw with such momentum that it was carried into the central pier.

His train dashed into the Norwalk River that empties into Long Island Sound. Forty-six passengers perished. The crew survived by jumping clear at the last minute. Feeling against the engineer at the scene was so strong that he may only have survived lynching by the inability of the crowd to decide whether he should be shot or strung-up!

The circumstances of the accident triggered widespread consternation among the travelling public. At the time the Canadian legislature was drafting a "Railways Protection Act," aimed at imposing a few elementary safety requirements on the modest, but growing, number of railway schemes.

Section VI of the Act, passed in 1853, was explicitly inserted as a direct consequence of the Norwalk tragedy. It stated:

> And be it enacted, That in all cases where Railroads pass any Draw or Swing Bridge over any navigable River, Canal or Stream which is subject to being opened for the purposes of navigation, the Trains shall in all and every case be stopped at least three minutes to ascertain from the bridge Tender that the said Bridge is closed and in perfect order for passing, and in default of so stopping during the full three minutes the said Railway Company shall be subject to a fine or penalty of One Hundred Pounds.

Such was the fear of any recurrence of such a fearful event that the Canadian government was prepared to exact a penalty that would exceed the entire revenue of a passenger train running between Toronto and Hamilton should such a train fail to halt a full three minutes at the drawbridge over the Desjardins Canal. While the Desjardins catastrophe could in no way be linked to negligence in the setting of the bridge, and, in fact, could be largely ascribed to bad fortune, it is nevertheless highly probable that had the train come to a full halt at the bridge approach the accident would not have occurred.

How did it come about that the Great Western appeared able to scorn with impunity the will of Parliament? Quite simply, because it obtained an extension to its own charter that permitted it to do so.

The 1855 act amending the company's charter containing Section XXIV was quoted earlier. In light of its incredible wording and momentous impact is worth repeating in full:

> And whereas it is doubtful whether the sixth section of the Statute passed in the sixteenth year of Her Majesty's Reign, instituted, An Act in addition to the general Railway Clauses Consolidation Act, was intended to apply to the Great Western Railway; And whereas the only draw-bridges on the line of the said Railway are so situated in regard to their proximity to Stations, and other circumstances, that it is not considered necessary that the said sixth section of the said Act should apply to the said Railway: Be it therefore enacted and declared, that the said sixth section of the said last mentioned Act was not intended to apply, nor shall the same apply or be in force in regard to the said Great Western Railway, in so far as respects to the Bridge over the Desjardins Canal, nor to any swing-bridge whilst the navigation is closed; any thing in the said Act contained to the contrary notwithstanding.

Incredible! Not only does an act of Parliament absolve one single company from a law that applied to all companies, but it is worded so as to suggest that the original legislation can't ever possibly have been intended to apply to that particular railway, and certainly not with respect to that railway's crossing of the Desjardins Canal.

How did the legislation that absolved the Great Western from the rule come about? The Great Western was seeking legislative authority to double its single track mainline. It turned to Samuel

Zimmerman to employ his influence in acquiring the necessary legislative approval. For his services, Zimmerman demanded and received from the Great Western the first right of refusal on the construction contract. As an additional favour he lobbied for the inclusion of the infamous Section XXVI into the act, empowering the track expansion. The double tracking was not undertaken at that time, so Zimmerman did not profit from that particular intervention. But the act stood and trains were no longer required to halt three minutes at the Desjardins Canal. The accident was not averted and Samuel Zimmerman died.

While it is probably a safe bet that had the train come to a complete stop before proceeding onto the bridge the derailment would have become evident, and that even if the damaged locomotive had proceeded after stopping the collapse of the bridge would not likely have occurred, it does not follow that there was any inherent danger in abolishing the rule. Of course the highway death toll could be minimized by limiting speed to ten kilometres an hour — but the consequent time loss would simply not be an acceptable cost for most people. Since the event occurred outside the navigation season and the bridge was secured in the closed position, the rule intended to prevent the recurrence of a train running into an open draw was, in March 1857, completely irrelevant. The real issue is whether the bridge (regardless of whether it was fixed or movable) was safe. Every structure has its limits and it is never possible to engineer all structures to absolutely preclude any possibility of a worse case outcome.

Certainly, when one looks at photographs of the bridge over the canal the design does seem fragile. Looks, however, can be deceiving. Since bridge building in North America was still in relative infancy there were many bridges constructed by well-intentioned carpenters that gave every appearance of solidity, but that nevertheless collapsed. Even in the 1870s an average of forty bridges of all descriptions fell in the United States — one for every four constructed each year. Was the Desjardins Bridge adequate to meet normal expected stress? Could it have been designed to remain intact under the circumstances that actually developed? If it could have been, should it have been built to those specifications?

Those are tricky questions. The answers have to be considered in the context of what was known about construction at the time. In other words, even if demonstrably insufficient under the circumstances, was it nevertheless state of the art for its time?

In the wake of the 1876 Ashtabula disaster the American Society of Civil Engineers roundly criticized the design of the bridge, arguing that such a structure should have been entrusted to a more qualified engineer, such as Squire Whipple, Albert Fink, or J.H. Linville.

Squire Whipple (Squire being his name and not a title) has been widely recognized as the father of scientific bridge building. Born in 1804 in Hardwick, Massachusetts, Whipple graduated from Union College in Schenectady, New York, and was subsequently employed as an engineer on the Erie Canal and a number of American railroads. A number of weight-efficient truss bridge designs had been introduced by William Howe, Thomas Pratt, and Ithiel Town (the latter being noted for a popular design for which he charged royalties of a dollar a linear foot if permission had been applied for — or two dollars a foot if he found out afterward). In 1846 Whipple (who already held a patent for an arched truss) introduced a design that became a classic in railroad history. The overall shape was trapezoidal — that is, the upper chord was shorter than the lower, or deck, chord, resulting in the end pieces being inclined toward the centre of the span. The sides were of complex lattice construction, with each diagonal crossing two panels.

The result was a strong, lightweight structure that was versatile, easily constructed, and could take advantages of the properties of cast iron (used in the posts and top chords) and wrought iron for the other members. In 1852–53 the first significant iron railroad bridge was built in West Troy, New York. The 146-foot span on the Rensselaer and Saratoga Railroad was a typical Whipple truss.

Although his bridges became common sights, Whipples's true claim to fame lay in his scientific approach to design and construction.

In 1847 he published his first book on the subject, and over the next thirty-five years or so various revisions were published. In *An Elementary and Practical Treatise on Bridge Building*, Whipple examined every design component and provided calculations that would enable designers to determine the weakest points in their structures. He discussed the merits of various construction materials and even factored into his comparisons the borrowing costs associated with higher-cost components.

Impressive as the achievements were, the greatest contribution of Whipples's methods is that they allowed scientific calculations of the margins of safety that could be built into bridges. Civil engineers have traditionally designed structures to withstand stresses and strains well in excess of the maximums that they were ever likely to encounter. Today a factor of ten is by no means unusual — that is, failure could only be expected when it is exposed to ten times the outside greatest expected load.

Retrospectively a committee of the Ohio legislature concluded that the Ashtabula Bridge had a safety factor of between 1.2 and 1.6. That meant it should have held up under a 20 to 60 percent excess above its maximum design load; against the crashing effect of derailed wheels dropping between the ties that proved to be patently insufficient.

Squire Whipple, armed with a truly scientific understanding of the loads his bridges could be expected to encounter and where the strains would be greatest, could design bridges that were cost efficient, strong where they needed to be, and light weight where extra material would simply be dead weight. He preferred a safety margin of ten times.

What could the sagacious pioneer of engineering prudence have to do with the corner-cutting Samuel Zimmerman, contractor for the Great Western? Zimmerman was well along the path to riches and influence before he was out of his twenties. Whipple didn't even start his engineering career until his thirties. They were unlikely collaborators, but it was to Squire Whipple that Zimmerman turned to design and build the bridge over the Desjardins Canal.

Perhaps Zimmerman's experience with the Niagara Suspension Bridge convinced him that whatever benefit might accrue from skimping on overall construction quality, it would be false economy to build failure-prone bridges. If so, he didn't apply the same logic to the notoriously unstable trestles he built. Perhaps Whipple's versatile design allowed him to price his expertise advantageously. That may indeed be the reason for purchasing the services of such an eminent engineer. After all, the bridge commissioned from Whipple was not one of the iron spans for which he was making a name for himself. Although adhering to Whipple's trapezoidal design, it was built of timber. To use Whipple's own phrase: the timbers were of "full medium quality when they were first put in."

In the context of the times there was absolutely nothing wrong with a wooden bridge. By far the majority of bridges were built of wood, and when properly designed and maintained they were certainly as safe as the often flawed iron structures available at the time. They did, however, have a much shorter expected life span than iron spans, and they did require greater vigilance, since they had a tendency to wear and weather quickly. The movement of the bridge under heavy traffic loosened boltholes and allowed water to penetrate. Wooden bridges had to be constantly tightened and rotting members had to be replaced.

Whipple clearly had a preference for iron, however, he claimed:

> But wood, though generally inferior in strength and durability, is much cheaper and lighter, so that making up with quantity for want of strength, and by frequent renewals, its want of durability, it has hereto been almost universally used in this country [United States] for bridge building; and in the scarcity of means, and the unsettled state of things in a new country, where improvements are necessarily, to a great extent of a temporary character,

this is undoubtedly the most economical material for the purpose.

In other words, if you couldn't afford better (and the Great Western certainly couldn't) then wood was a perfectly acceptable material.

The wood employed was white pine. After the disaster some claimed that the original specifications called for the use of oak and that Zimmerman surreptitiously substituted pine. It makes for a good tale, but oak wasn't the wood of choice. Although the durability and strength of oak have become almost legendary, most North American oak is knotty, cross-grained, and "season-checked." While inherently weaker per foot, certain varieties of pine are generally considered the strongest timbers available in the lengths typically required in bridge construction. So pine was the safer choice.

And safety was clearly a factor in the case of the Desjardins Bridge. Although Zimmerman was the contractor, the design specifications would have been originally drafted and the plans would have required the approval of the Great Western's engineer in 1853, T. Clarke. Whipple claimed that the engineer's instructions were "to make the primary and paramount object to consist in the safety and the sufficiency of the structure, as to strength, with as great a degree of attention to the case of convenience of working it as a drawbridge as might be consistent with the more important consideration of strength and stability as a bridge for railroad purposes." Whipple argued that the form of trussing used in the bridge "… has been theoretically demonstrated, I think beyond reasonable dispute, to combine strength and lightness to a greater degree than any other form in use."

The bridge was designed with a sixteen-foot platform above the turntable and eight nine-foot sections for the seventy-two-foot span northward over the canal, and four nine-foot sections forming the counterbalance on the south side of the turntable over land. The height was eighteen feet.

After the accident, widespread doubts about the sufficiency of the bridge were raised. Understandably, many felt that it was self evident that a bridge that collapsed under a train was just not properly built and, of course, against the abysmal safety record of the Great Western such arguments quickly gained currency. Political impartiality was not a strongpoint of the press of the day and some papers, such as William Lyon Mackenzie's *Weekly Record* and the *Toronto Leader*, were fulsome in their attacks against railways that took the lives of their passengers so lightly.

Mackenzie rushed into print within days of the disaster to assert:

> Without waiting for more testimony, we hesitate not to state our opinion that the swing bridge, as built, was weak and unsafe; that it was discreditable to the engineer who superintended its erection, and to all who succeeded to his office; that it was the duty of the resident directors, and especially of the manager, Mr. Brydges, to have examined this dangerous, unsafe structure, situated close to their very doors, and which had shown symptoms of decay but a short time previous, and to have a first class engineer constantly on the works, with his experienced eye on the rolling stock, the rails, the bridges etc., even if his ample salary had diminished by a cent in the dollar the annual dividends of a few Lombard Street Israelites.

The bombastic and anti-Semitic allegations of the explosive Lyon Mackenzie notwithstanding, the issue of the bridge's safety was a critical concern and would demand a good deal of time at the Coroner's Inquest.

CHAPTER NINE

THE INQUEST

The role of government in the 1850s was much less encompassing than it is today. One might expect judicial investigations prior to Confederation to have been rather cursory affairs, but it was quite the opposite. Although nearly all court appointments were part-time and resources were clearly limited, quite elaborate investigations could still be mounted. The loss of so many prominent lives evidently spurred authorities into immediate action. With the reputation of the Great Western already deeply tarnished by the earlier findings of the Legislative Commission of Inquiry into the alarming frequency of accidents on the railway, the Desjardins disaster demanded a comprehensive inquiry.

From the orderly manner in which the casualties were registered, through the evidence taken in the inquiry and the deliberations of the jury, the Canadian respect of due process was evident. Even by modern standards the inquest was painstakingly diligent and above board. A scale model of the bridge itself was also built and exhibited in court, and the commissioner of Public Works hired photographer R. Milne to detail the condition of the bridge and track as well as the damaged rolling stock. That evidence was used in the ensuing enquiry. Incidentally, the government eventually balked at meeting Milne's invoice when presented, arguing that £36 was too high. The court ordered payment of £22, a partial victory for the government achieved with only a modest additional investment of £41 in legal fees!

Coroners H.R. Bull and Dr. J.A.W. Rosebrugh were immediately on the job. John Wellington Rosebrugh, although only twenty-nine years old at the time, had completed his initial medical training only five years earlier, but had already augmented his credentials by further studies in New York and Toronto, and had served as Wentworth County coroner before being appointed in Hamilton. In part, he had honed his early surgical skills by patching together the wounds experienced by brawling railway navies and

This composite image was published by the Morning Banner *of Buffalo, New York, based on the "ambrotype" by local photographer R. Milne. Although photography was still in its infancy, authorities made substantial use of the technique to capture the technical aspects of the disaster as well as the images of the unidentified corpses. As this illustration shows, the media were also exploring the technique to sell newspapers. By the time there was sufficient light the following morning, the delicately balanced car had been demolished, so the publisher simply added it back in, along with the staged observers.*

LIBRARY AND ARCHIVES CANADA, C41060.

The Inquest

amputating limbs mangled during the construction and primitive operating regime of the Great Western.

The coroners' first responsibilities had been to identify as many of the corpses laid out in the freight depot and baggage rooms at the Great Western works as possible. Not surprisingly, since the railways had opened long-distance travel to the masses, there were a fair number of unidentified bodies. Who knew how long it would take to track down the identity of each of them? Predictably, some identities were never established. Since it might be weeks or months before reports of someone being missing from a distant town might reach Hamilton, a novel approach was adopted: photography. Not to be outdone by the Public Works commissioner, the Great Western also contracted Milne to take pictures of each unidentified body, apparently the first time such a thing had been done. The decision to photograph the remains showed astonishingly enlightened judgment.

On Friday, March 13, the day after the accident, the coroner's jury was empanelled in the boardroom of the Great Western Railway on Hamilton's King Street. As was customary in the case of multiple deaths in a single incident, they were directed to inquire into how one person, in this case Donald Stuart (the city alderman) and "many others" met their deaths. Again following custom, their first task was to retire to the railway sheds to view the bodies. They then adjourned until 2:00 p.m. on Saturday.

The task of the jury was straightforward. There was no doubt as to how the victims died. They died when the train broke through the bridge and crashed to the ice. The essential question to be answered, however, was whether the bridge was designed and maintained in a manner that would be perfectly safe except under extreme circumstances, such as a derailment, or whether the bridge was inherently unsafe and just collapsed under the simple stress of a normal crossing.

From the beginning the railway contended that the engine somehow became derailed at the switch that was placed just 130 feet north of the bridge. Being off the track when it reached the bridge it fell upon the cross ties, subjecting them to a totally unplanned stress, and at the same time, it was conjectured, canted over and destroyed a part of the latticework that held the top and bottom chords together. Under such circumstances, it was argued, no bridge could conceivably be designed to withstand the effects.

The jury's task can be crystallized into the following: a) Was the bridge inherently unsafe and liable to collapse under the normal load of traffic? b) Was the accident the result of an unanticipatable stress being imposed on an otherwise entirely safe structure? c) Could the bridge have been designed in a manner that would have provided greater safety, even in the event of an engine or train being derailed?

The latter, perhaps understandably, occupied little of the jury's time. To build a bridge actually designed to withstand a substantial multiple of its anticipated maximum normal stress was itself radical enough; to design one that could withstand the excesses of a catastrophic event would have been revolutionary. In later years the track on bridges would be augmented by an additional pair of "check" rails, mounted inside the normal rails that would prevent the engine or car from slewing across the track whenever one wheel was derailed. If the idea had been applied anywhere, it certainly was not the practice on the Great Western. Had it been, it likely would have made little difference, unless the cross ties were very much closer together.

The rails were laid directly onto fourteen-foot-wide ties (or needle beams) that were approximately seven by seven inches in cross-section. These were attached below the longitudinal beams parallel to the tracks (stringers) and together formed the floor of the bridge. The gaps between the ties might originally have been as much as four feet. Although the installation of an additional twelve needle beams in August 1856 would have narrowed those gaps, the space between them would still have been large enough that the leading wheels of a locomotive that was off the rails would easily slip down between them. The setup is similar to riding a bicycle over a horizontal ladder. If the rungs are close enough together, it is quite simple. If they are spaced wider apart it would be hopeless. The ties on the bridge were impossibly widely spaced. Once the engine wheel slipped into the

The Inquest

opening, all of the momentum of the train would be concentrated at that point. If the beam did not shatter then the train would instantly pile up behind the engine. If it did shatter then the engine would sink further through the gap and encounter the next beam as it continued its forward momentum.

Clearly, a solid plank floor would enable a locomotive to stay on the bridge even if it were off the rails. Unless the jury felt that such a safety feature as a solid floor should have been installed (despite it being uncommon), then the issue was reduced to whether or not the bridge was safe under usual traffic.

The railway's job was to demonstrate the excess safety margin built into the design and the rigour with which the structure was maintained. To that end they made sure that a steady stream of expert witnesses were made available to the coroner's jury. Two civil engineers were attached to the investigation, John T. Clarke and Thomas Keefer. From later legislative records it would appear their participation was at public cost.

Both their reports generally exonerated the company. Neither would have had particular affection for the railway, so their finding should be judged as reasonably impartial. Clarke, of course, was the engineer who resigned his position on the Great Western in 1854 when C.J. Brydges ignored his written concerns over the unsafe conditions that prevailed when the line opened. He subsequently took the position of state engineer and surveyor general for the State of New York — the position he still held when he participated in the inquiry.

The other, Thomas Keefer, along with his brother, Samuel Keefer, enjoyed illustrious careers as notable Canadian civil engineers. Between them they were engaged in a number of railway and bridge projects. Thomas was a rather testy and self-opinionated man. His proposals for the Victoria Bridge at Montreal were rejected in favour of those of the more famous Robert Stevenson. With what degree of justice can no longer be determined, he took his claim to have been unfairly compensated by the Grand Trunk for his contribution all the way to the legislature.

Thomas Keefer was not universally applauded. The *Toronto Leader* (a pro-government, pro-Grand Trunk newspaper), long before his appearance at the inquest mounted a scathing attack on his professional qualifications that included the following vituperative gem:

> In these days of political excitement we have not always given time and space to the efforts after notoriety of such men as Mr. Thomas Keefer, who in his attack on the Grand Trunk Railway, resembles as much as anything we know, the fly on the wheel, with this difference, that while the ambitious little insect congratulated himself on the progress he was making, our would-be arbiter is pluming himself on his power to annihilate a great national enterprise. His efforts however, tend no little to show his utter disqualification for the position to which he aspires.

What followed was a lot more in the same vein.

Doubtless Keefer was a bit of a martinet and he took every opportunity that presented itself to vent his umbrage in letters to the editor of many newspapers.

Thomas Keefer was responsible for the design of the municipal waterworks in Montreal, Ottawa, and Hamilton. Whether any of the attacks on his engineering qualifications were justified can no longer be gauged, but the massive stone pumphouse designed to supply water to Hamilton in 1859 remains an outstanding example of Victorian elegance and durability. It was refurbished several decades ago and is open as a public exhibit.

Keefer was a strong critic of the Great Western's construction. A half-dozen years after the disaster he railed against the "engineer who located the road," suggesting that he "had a weakness for straight lines." Keefer argued that the line was driven along the surveyed course without reference to the fact that a slight deviation would have avoided unnecessary bridgework, and was especially critical of the Hamilton layout that benefited MacNab but involved so much heavy engineering along the Dundas side of the escarpment.

He saved some of his sharpest barbs for Samuel Zimmerman. It was Keefer who, without naming him, tagged Zimmerman as "one bold operator" who "organized a system which virtually made him ruler of the province for several years." Of Zimmerman's death, Keefer after telling how the legislation requiring trains to stop at the bridge was rescinded, wrote: "In less than two years thereafter, a train which did not stop plunged through this very bridge and among the first recovered of the sixty victims to that 'accident' was the dead body of the great contractor himself."

Those words written in 1863 reflect poorly on Keefer as an individual. The inclusion of the word "accident" within quotation marks could only be read as implying that the disaster might in some way be a result of negligence. Although in his own official report in 1857 Keefer was careful to avoid commenting on the "sufficiency" of the bridge, and while he did suggest that it could have been more effectively designed, he nevertheless concluded that "any wooden bridge with the roadway upon the lower chords would have shared a similar fate."

Among the many grudges that Keefer appeared to nurse it is probable that he had a burning resentment toward Samuel Zimmerman. At one point Keefer's father, Jacob Keefer, invested heavily in milling, having built operations on the Welland Canal at Thorold that were capable of grinding two to three hundred barrels a day. Unfortunately, before the mills were completed the preferential tariff afforded Canadian flour under the British corn laws was abolished and Jacob Keefer was obliged to heavily mortgage the operations. He lost control of the mills in 1850 and the mortgage holders eventually foreclosed in 1855. Who were the mortgagors? Samuel Zimmerman and his partner James Oswald!

The first day of evidence was on Saturday, March 14th. Less than forty-eight hours after the accident, at two in the afternoon, the jury met in the courthouse. The first to testify was Edward Levier, the baggageman who had been perched on top of some luggage piled up near the open door on the side of the baggage car facing away from the lake. He testified that he heard the sharp brake whistle and instantly saw the engine "sink through the bridge." He was not able to shed much more light on the circumstances. He felt no jolting as if the train was off the tracks but was simply aware of the engine passing on to the bridge and the instantaneous descent of the bridge and engine — before even the tender left the abutment. That was all.

Levier, however, was the first to mention yet another coincidence. Just about a month earlier an axle broke on a locomotive as it ran onto the bridge. No one was hurt and the cars remained on the bridge, but seventeen of the needle beams had to be replaced since eleven were broken and six chipped.

Later on that first day of the inquest one of the bridge tenders dropped a further bombshell. In June of the previous year there had been yet another derailment on the bridge. On that occasion the train had got over safely but the gouge left on the tie showed that the leading wheel of the locomotive had come within one inch of the edge. Disaster had been narrowly averted on that occasion. The name of that locomotive that had such a narrow escape was Oxford — the same engine that was still lying upside down in the mud and frigid waters beneath the Desjardins Canal.

Over the next two days witnesses added to the weight of evidence that the engine was clearly off the track before it reached the bridge. There really could be no doubt whatsoever — the proof was writ clear on the approaches. At the switch, just 130 feet from the canal, a one-and-a-half-inch iron connecting rod was cut clear through, and another just below it was gouged. On the ties leading up to the bridge blue/grey marks on the wood traced a path, and on the abutment itself was the clear scrape of metal on stone. If no bridge could reasonably be expected to withstand the strain of a derailed train and if the evidence was clear that on March 12th the engine was clearly off the tracks, then the event was an unavoidable disaster in which negligence played no part. Among those testifying to that effect were the train's conductor and William Muir, the assistant superintendent of the line, who happened to have been on board.

By the fourth day of the inquest, Wednesday, March 18th, the focus was switching toward questions about the maintenance and adequacy of the bridge. Current and former employees who shared responsibility for the upkeep of the span testified about how they performed their duties. James Sergeant, a past inspector of bridges on the line, testified that he had switched the pine longitudinal stringers from pine to oak and added some crossties, and was afterward satisfied with the safety of the structure. He also introduced a slightly discordant note in his comments. "When the bridge was being put up it looked slight," he testified, adding that he wouldn't cross until he had seen an engine pass over. Sergeant claimed to have told the designer, Whipple, that he considered the timbers "slight" and commented that a "slight bridge requires more attention than a heavy one."

The bridge did look flimsy. That could hardly be in dispute. As noted in the preceding chapter, however, bridges at the time were constructed rather than designed. A massively built structure might impart confidence in its sturdiness while still being structurally unsound from an engineering perspective. The real issue was whether it was intrinsically strong, no matter what appearance it gave. Richard Bond, the Great Western's then-inspector of bridges thought it was. With twenty years experience he felt himself "able to judge when a bridge is right or wrong," and he claimed he always felt that the bridge was safe.

On Monday, March 23rd, a crowd of more than a thousand gathered at the canal in anticipation of the raising of the locomotive. The engine was slowly winched to the surface and there, in view of the jury, the city council, a bevy of engineers, and a smattering of reporters, was shown the evidence that confirmed what had been widely suspected. The leading right-hand wheel of the four-wheeled "truck" at the very front of the engine was missing. Moreover, it was clear that the axle had broken near the wheel and an examination showed that the end was worn — implying that it must have fractured sometime before reaching the bridge.

The following day additional testimony was presented to show that the bridge was sufficiently strong. Anthony Sherwood, an engineer on the Buffalo, Brantford & Goderich Railway had calculated that the bridge would withstand four and a half times its normal maximum load. He felt that seasoned pine was preferable to oak, and he had not observed any "brashy" timbers in the bridge.

When the jury reassembled at 8:00 p.m. that same day, Andrew Talcott, chief engineer on the Ohio and Mississippi Railroad, reported on his examination of the remains of the bridge. He estimated that the bridge was strong enough to support three times the maximum anticipated load, and added that such a margin was as great as one might find on the majority of American railroads. Citing his West Point education and eighteen years experience as a military engineer, Talcott boldly stated that he did not know of "a single bridge in America that would stand when such a force of impact should come in contact with it."

William Garrick was the foreman of the crew that replaced the needle beams after the February accident. He too asserted that the bridge was in good shape and that the repairs had restored the bridge to full strength. He believed that the locomotive and train would not have broken through so long as they remained on the rails. He was in a good position to judge, since not only did he supervise the repairs, he also had a ringside seat at the disaster. Garrick was one of the lucky few occupying the first car of the train on March 12th who lived to recount his experience. Not only did he live, he was catapulted into the water and escaped serious injury.

On March 25th, the eighth day of the inquiry, a further excursion was planned to examine the wreck of the locomotive in greater detail. This was aborted when news arrived that the chains had snapped and Oxford had, once again, slipped to the bottom of the canal.

In place of the trip to the canal, a special train was laid on (actually a special car attached to the end of a freight train) and the jurors were taken to Thorold, where a similar, although shorter, bridge spanned the Welland Canal.

The Inquest

Sometimes an element of humour creeps into the grimmest of proceedings. The engineering naïveté of the doubtless well-intentioned jurors proved too much for the local correspondent of the *Toronto Leader*. He couldn't resist having fun at their expense.

The day was wet, windy, and cold and the jurors must have found it unpleasant to be evicted from the warmth of the train to face a chilly scramble over the slippery timbers of the bridge, accompanied by the ever-present prospect of a misstep throwing them into the canal. They appear, however, to have accepted the challenge with gusto.

According to the *Leader*'s reporter:

> One juror shook the bridge with all his might, and seemed not a little astonished that he did not displace at least two or three of the timbers; another no less zealous juror beat the timbers with his knuckles until they ached (his knuckles not the timbers) but left off without coming to any satisfactory result; a third made strenuous efforts to remove an iron bolt with his walking stick, and did not desist until the walking stick gave unmistakable signs of parting in two; a fourth and fifth came near dancing a jig on the centre of the bridge, by way of trying its strength, only that owing to the absence of planking, the possibilities of a broken neck or drowning were to be set off against the possibility of the bridge breaking.

There was a good deal of measuring and estimating — especially when a long freight train trundled over. Eventually two heavy locomotives were brought up to give the jury an opportunity to examine the bridge under maximum stress. According to the *Leader* report, this was accompanied by a fair deal of drama as the engines were several times driven to the edge of the bridge and then backed up, only to approach again. Eventually the coupled engines were run out on the bridge and the jurors were able to judge the deflection the weight caused in the structure. A comparison of notes showed that the effect of the massive weight was to cause the bridge to sag something between three-eighths of an inch to three inches. That being too vague an estimate, the exercise was repeated with one adventurous juror scrambling under the bridge just beside the abutment and taking a measurement with the aid of two walking sticks! The conclusion of this experiment was that the deflection was around three-eighths of an inch, which would be somewhat greater at the middle of the bridge and even greater on the longer span over the Desjardins Canal. This information apparently served little purpose, since no one present seemed to know whether that degree of sag was normal or extreme.

The writer for the *Leader* noted the absence of the Crown prosecutor who had been assigned to the inquiry. "His presence would not have served any good purpose as he frankly admitted that he did not understand anything at all about engineering or bridges." The journalist went on to suggest that "he knew probably as much as the majority of those who were present did, on the same subjects."

The next day, March 26th, the inquest heard from the star witness, Squire Whipple himself. Although an experienced engineer, and author of a major treatise on bridge construction, Whipple had not yet achieved the widespread acclaim as the "father of scientific bridge design" that he would later in life. In the mistrustful mood that persisted just two weeks after the accident, there were those who remained antagonistic toward the "Yankee" engineer. Yet the calm, thoughtful, and meticulous submission of the bridge's builder must have done much to influence the public mood.

Whipple had spent the better part of the preceding week examining the wreckage and preparing a formal report. While shedding substantial light on the details of the design, Whipple's official remarks must have imposed a heavy burden on those jurors without technical expertise who were bound to sit though the reading. Longwinded sentences and turgid prose, interspersed with technical terminology and wave after wave of cautious equivocation must have left many of his audience lost.

Nevertheless, stripped of the verbiage, the message must have been very clear. Squire Whipple was a supremely logical, cautious, and scrupulous engineer whose instructions had been "to make the primary and paramount object to consist in the safety and sufficiency of the structure, as to strength." At every step in the process Whipple had clearly satisfied himself that he had complied with that mandate. Some witnesses had relied on the fact that the structure had stood for three years as prima facie evidence that the design was sound. At a time when railroad bridges were only expected to last about nine years before major renewal, perhaps that was a reasonable proposition; but not for Whipple. For him, a structure had to pass both the theoretical validity of design as well as the demonstrated practical qualities of stability and durability.

The step-by-step procedures he applied to the engineering of the Desjardins Canal Bridge, and to bridge design in general, were spelled out in full detail for the jurors. With the aid of diagrams and a scale model of the bridge, he tried to guide them along his thoroughly logical approach.

First, he selected the overall style of the bridge. This was no difficult task for him, since he was confident that the "Whipple truss" — comprised of upper and lower chords joined by diagonal truss work — was demonstrably the most efficient. In fact, he claimed that it had been theoretically demonstrated "… to combine strength with lightness, to a greater degree than any other form in use."

The next step was to determine the overall dimensions. The bridge had to be high enough to provide clearance for the exaggerated smokestacks of wood-burning locomotives (eighteen feet) and the side panels had to be no longer than eight to ten feet in order to provide the necessary support. Since the bridge was to be constructed with two arms attached to the sixteen-foot turntable, he settled on panels of approximately nine feet wide.

Given the overall dimensions, Whipple next turned his attention to the combination of size and proportion of the various elements and the construction material. At this stage in his report he launched into a detailed exposition of the various qualities of white pine when subjected to the different directions of stress that are encountered in bridgework, along with the necessary adjustments that have to be taken into account when the timber is drilled where the bolts pass through. The objective of all these precise calculations was to enable all the components to "perform their functions with about the same ease, safety and certainty, without lumbering it with useless weight in unimportant parts." Whipple's approach was quite the contrast to the prevailing methodology of producing structures that only *looked* substantial. For Whipple, it was important that so long as every part was properly designed to meet the actual demand expected of it, then the next consideration would be for it to be as light as possible. If indeed the bridge inspector had commented to Whipple that the design appeared "slight," the latter might well have taken that as a compliment.

With the virtue of historical perspective, it is easy to see why Whipple came to be recognized for contributing so much to "modern" bridge design. His approach injected true scientific reasoning into engineering. But no matter how progressive his thinking, his presentations must have tortured his audience. The sense of the mind-numbing detail Whipple provided in his report can be garnered from a single quotation representative of many such observations. Referencing labelled parts of a schematic diagram of the bridge, he stated: "The next diagonal NH composed of 2 pieces, 3 1/4 by 6 inches, suffers 6,345 lbs. thrust, only 162 lb. to the square inch, with D loaded and N unloaded, a tension of 2,115 lbs. with the load reversed, and a thrust of 4,230 lbs. with both these points full loaded, with the assumed full load of 12,000 lbs. to each." To jurors who attempted to measure bridge deflection with the aid of walking sticks, Whipple's testimony must have been completely incomprehensible.

Perhaps that was not entirely unintentional. The ambition of the railway was to demonstrate the meticulous planning and attention to detail that had gone into the design and construction of the bridge. To that end, Whipple made an impressive contribution. Under questioning, he refused to rely simply on his design calculations to assert the structure's margin of strength. He recognized that some of the timbers would have deteriorated with age, but was still willing to claim that the bridge would have sustained a weight of 400 tons, while the maximum weight that normal traffic could impose would be just seventy-two tons.

The thorough analysis and conservative claims of the engineer must have added considerable conviction to his conclusion.

> From what proceeds, it is abundantly evident to me, that the bridge over the Desjardins Canal was not broken by the simple pressure of traffic passing over it bearing on the track and rails; and it is my decided opinion ... that the immediate cause of the disaster on the 12th instant, was the violent collision of some part or parts of the locomotive attached to the ill-fated train with the timbers of the ill-fated bridge....

Whipple's work was done and the Great Western seemed well on the road to exoneration.

The next time the jury met, on Monday, March 30th, they dedicated several hours to a thorough examination of the locomotive, which had been safely returned to dry land. They then adjourned until the following day, when various maintenance staff reported on recent repairs to Oxford. Driver Burnfield had reported various defects, the only one requiring immediate attention being the iron tire attached to the right-hand driving wheel. Oxford was in the Hamilton shops from January 20th until March 6th. The repair log was introduced into evidence showing repairs to the pilot, pistons, eccentric rod, gauge taps, wheels, and tires. The axles were apparently not replaced at the time, but were subjected to examination — visually and by sounding with a hammer. Had any defect been suspected the axle would have been heated to check for differences in appearance. All concerned declared that Oxford was, for all practical purposes, as good as new when it left the shops. Less than a week later, after clocking just 347 miles, Oxford was at the bottom of the Desjardins Canal.

On the Friday, the inquest reconvened to hear John McAlpine, the engineer for the railway's eastern division and the man with primary responsibility for the bridge. His calculations led him to believe that even after making allowance for any imperfections in material or workmanship the ratio of ultimate strength to greatest load to be three and three quarters to one. As with so many other witnesses, he concluded that "There are degrees of safety in different bridges, but supposing a locomotive off the tracks they are all on a par."

So far the Great Western had things its own way. Every effort to maintain the locomotive had been taken, but an undetectable fault had caused it to leave the tracks just as it was entering the bridge. The bridge was well designed and properly maintained, and no other bridge could have withstood the tremendous shock of a derailment occurring where, by sheer misfortune, it did. But the tide was about to turn. The testimony began to become more condemnatory and the outcome of the inquest must have appeared uncertain.

To the stand came Frederick Preston Rubidge, assistant engineer of Public Works. Rubidge hadn't been brought in by the Great Western, he has been appointed by the assistant commissioner of Public Works to report to the government on the condition of the bridge. He concluded that the bridge has been in an unsound, unsafe, and dangerous condition on and before March 12, 1857.

His report was lengthy and devastating. He faulted the design of the bridge and its condition. He felt the bridge was longer than it needed to be, that the overall design was unfavourable, that the suspension of the needle beams below the longitudinal stringers was ill-advised, that the repairs after the February accident had been made with inferior wood, and that the whole structure was compromised by rot and severe chaffing around the bolt holes. He identified two distinct positions at which the longitudinal stringers were vulnerable to failure and went so far as to introduce a handful of the decayed wood to the court. His report described the bracing at one of the failure points as showing "… a deadened cross-grained fibre, which a common place remark, 'short as a carrot' so well illustrates, that I here insert it."

By Rubidge's calculations the condition of the bridge was such that it could just barely carry the maximum weight of normal traffic, but was utterly incapable of dealing with any sort of extreme stress.

A certain animosity was evident in the questioning by the company representative. Was the witness aware that a similar bridge spanned the Welland Canal? If you found that to be sound, would you conceive your opinion erroneous? "I don't say the Desjardins Bridge was unsafe — I merely calculate that it would be so if theory is correct." That doesn't get him off the hook.

"Do you found your report merely on theory?" queries the company agent.

Rubidge counters that he compares his theory with results on other bridges, much stronger than this.

Perhaps a sharper point is made when the same interrogator asks about his credentials and elicits the response that he "… never had any training as a civil engineer beyond that which 30 years' experience gives. The most celebrated engineers are those who commenced in this way." The coroners cut off further questioning in this vein, but whatever the witness might lack in diplomas that handful of decayed wood must have made its mark.

The chief virtue of Rubidge's testimony might have been that he was seemingly impartial — being a civil servant appointed by the government, rather than an expert whose expenses were covered by the Great Western. Such was the state of distrust, however, that the local press perceived him as an agent of Toronto interests and naturally prejudiced against the Hamilton enterprise. He was also forced to admit some miscalculations in his report — overestimating the weight of Oxford at twenty-eight tons instead of twenty-four and significantly underestimating the height of the smokestack. Despite these shortcomings, his report might have had a greater impact were it not for the next witness, a man under whose direction Rubridge had once worked — a man whose opinion carried more weight.

Thomas K. Keefer was also commissioned by the Crown. As noted earlier, Keefer may have been a little ungenerous in choosing not to comment on the "sufficiency" of the bridge. Had he designed the bridge he would arranged for trains to travel over the top of the structure rather than through the middle. While that would have made it easier to place the ties above the longitudinal beams (as opposed to the dubious choice of suspending them below) it could hardly have averted the loss of a train that actually derailed on the bridge. He did note that the very fact that as a swing bridge it had held up under traffic for three years without adjustment, implied something about its adequacy — but he cast a telling aspersion by noting that there was, in fact, no way of adjusting it. Other designs employed threaded iron rods to provide vertical stiffness. These could occasionally be tightened with the use of turnbuckles, whenever wear and tear loosened the side frames. Wooden latticework would chafe at pressure points and could only be tightened by inserting packing material.

Squire Whipple was not ignorant of the benefits of iron elements. In his 1847 book he took the trouble to compute the monetary advantages of the two materials. By his calculations a wood structure would have to be completely replaced every nine years. If a suitable capital fund was established that would generate the necessary funds for replacement, then he could calculate how much it would cost to maintain the bridge in perpetuity. Calculations for a comparable iron structure, requiring less frequent replacement, demonstrated that over the longer term iron was significantly more cost-effective. Of course, the Great Western didn't have capital to spare and it was more expedient to build in wood and worry about replacement costs after the railway started generating revenue. Although Whipple was adamant that properly planned and maintained wooden structures were entirely adequate, his own designs, along with those of other bridge engineers, increasingly favoured iron.

The Inquest

While Keefer would neither endorse nor condemn the bridge, his main contribution to the inquiry was a detailed exposition of the probable course of events from the point where the leading wheels derailed at the switch, which he did by tracking the evidence left on the ties, the stone abutment, and the members of the bridge. He left no doubt at all that the cause of the accident was the derailment of the locomotive. For the Great Western, the testimony was highly satisfactory.

Thomas Coltrin Keefer appears every inch the dour civil engineer that his testimony suggests. Although he could not quite bring himself to actually fault the bridge's design or construction in his official report, his antipathy towards Zimmerman was evident in his out-of-court observations.

LIBRARY AND ARCHIVES CANADA, PA033952.

The Coroner charged the jury to find whether the bridge was adequate for normal traffic, taking into account design and maintenance, how any unusual strain came about, and whether, if that unusual strain occurred as a result of the broken axle, it was foreseeable or not. The jury was instructed that they could proffer charges of criminal negligence or manslaughter, and could impose a heavy "Deodand" upon the company. That was a remnant of ecclesiastical law providing that any inanimate object that was the cause of death could be surrendered to the court — or a fine in lieu thereof.

After a short adjournment the jury found the following: 1) the immediate cause of the accident was the breaking of the forward axle; 2) "Oxford" had undergone a thorough repair and was turned out in good and satisfactory condition, and had been properly examined before leaving Toronto; 3) the bridge was constructed of sufficient strength to convey traffic safely and securely, so long as it remained on the track; 4) the bridge was not sufficiently strong in the event the engine and cars were off the track.

The jurors recommended the replacement of the bridge with a permanent (i.e., fixed) bridge and that the former law requiring locomotives to come to a complete stop before crossing the Desjardins, or any other movable bridge, be reinstated. "Believing, as they do,

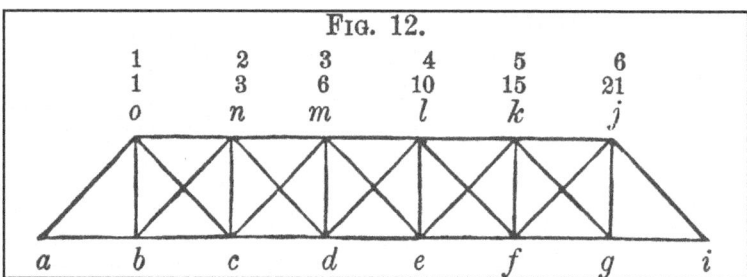

An illustration from Whipple's classic An Elementary and Practical Treatise on Bridge Building. *Illustrations were few in the 350-page volume and the text was heavy on formulae and measurements. The similarity with the failed canal bridge shown in the previous picture is obvious.*

NEW YORK: D. VAN NOSTRAND, 1873, 17.

that the lamentable accident might have been avoided had this precautionary measure remained in full force."

The accident "might have been avoided"! But it wasn't. Like all such occurrences, the tragedy was the confluence of events with trails woven through the history of the era. For Alex Burnfield the story perhaps began when he decided to leave his native Scotland on a path that would eventually lead to his hand being on the throttle of Oxford on March 12, 1857. For Samuel Zimmerman the journey may have commenced when he urged his mare and buggy over the border into Canada. Perhaps the course of history began when Pierre Desjardins first conceived a canal from Dundas to Burlington Bay, or when the aging Colonel Talbot turned the first sod of the Great Western near London. There were a multitude of beginnings all leading inexorably to one ending — a convergence from which sixty people would diverge no further.

Although the disaster was in every dimension a truly human tragedy, a dispassionate observer might also view it as a progression of purely physical events leading to an inevitable outcome. In such terms one might develop a chronology from a foundry in Schenectady, New York, to the bottom of the Desjardins Canal.

The faulty axle was almost certainly cast in Schenectady. The Great Western was experimenting with wheel castings at Hamilton and the railway shops were gearing up to take on the fabrication of most locomotive components, as well as the design and construction of entire engines, but had probably not begun casting axles. There is no way of knowing for sure whether the axle had ever been changed since the delivery of Oxford in 1854. That said, given the poor quality of the road bed and the constant jarring the rolling stock was subject to, to say nothing of the serious accidents the Oxford was known to have been involved in, it is quite likely that replacements had been necessary.

Wherever the axle started its career, deep inside the metal, invisible to the eye, there was almost certainly a flaw. That was a constant danger with primitive iron casting. The Great Western had experienced a good deal of difficulty with poor wheel castings, although the absence of commentary at the inquest into the early accidents suggests that the more massive axle castings may have given less trouble. Indeed, the shop foreman George Forsyth ventured in testimony that the incident might have been the first time a pilot axle failure had occurred "on the road."

Fully refurbished, resplendent in the company's green livery, and with fresh paint on the buffer bars, Oxford left the Hamilton repair shops on March 6th. Four trips to Copeland, a trip to London and back, and Oxford was reassigned to its regular Toronto-Hamilton run on March 11th. At Toronto, locomotive department foreman William Jenkins examined the working parts of the engine on the afternoon of the 12th. Engineer Burnfield and Fireman Knight would also have carried out an examination (apart from other motivations the engineer could have been charged the replacement cost of any part that overheated if it had not been properly oiled). That process would have entailed tapping each of the wheels with a long handled hammer. Faults in the metal could typically be detected by a dull sound in contrast to the brighter note of sound metal. That technique, however, could hardly be expected to reveal the flaw hidden within the axle.

At 4:10 Oxford pulled her train out of the Queen's Wharf station to begin her final trip. Through Mimico, Port Credit, Oakville, Bronte, Wellington Square, and Waterdown the train trundled. By the time it drew away from Waterdown its complement was complete. The Reverend Booker was on board; the fortunate traveller who had stepped down was left behind.

Throughout that journey the two ends of the axle were beginning to lose their grip. Somewhere between Waterdown and the switch one hundred thirty feet away from the end of the bridge the axle failed. Even though, at a molecular level, they were now entirely separate, it is probable that for a little while the two pieces rotated in unison, the wheels turning at the same rate. Then, perhaps barely perceptibly, the rotation would skip a turn, so that the two open ends would spin against each other, wearing the edges down a trifle and burnishing the broken ends.

Somewhere just before the switch, at about a quarter to six, the right-hand wheel, close to the break in the axle, would have began to take on an independent momentum — probably tilting outward under the weight of the pilot truck whilst constrained by the inside flange. The pilot, still supported by three wheels, might not immediately have shown outward signs of instability, but the free end of the axle would have begun to drop down into the right-of-way between the two rails. The left-hand leading wheel left the tracks around this point, falling between the rails.

What actually fouled the switch is not certain. It could have been either of the detached wheels or the free end of the axle attached to the left-hand wheel. But the switch was fouled. The left wheel severed a connecting rod and gouged another one lower down in the track bed. The wooden ties between the rails were scarred by the wheel's passage. There still may have been no obvious sign of a problem. The driving wheels was still on the track, the engine was travelling in the right direction, and whatever sounds emanating from the loose gear would have been drowned by the usual clanking and snorting of an old-fashioned steam engine.

At six miles an hour the engine would take about fifteen seconds to reach the edge of the bridge. By the time David Crombie, standing by the switch, briefly swung himself onto the platform at the end of the last car, the engine must have just about reached the bridge. The entire train has passed Crombie without him detecting anything amiss.

The stone abutment of the bridge stood a few inches higher between the rails than the preceding ties. In all likelihood, this was the point at which the fate of the entire train was sealed. As the derailed left-hand wheel came in contact with the unyielding limestone surface it would have heaved the weight of the engine upward, pushing the driving wheels off the rail. (The absence of any marks on the tie immediately in front of the abutment, despite deep scarring on the approaching ties, tends to confirm this course of events.) At this point the pilot truck slewed to the right, just as the engine moved onto the bridge. Burnfield had inches and split seconds in which to react; all he had time to do was blow the whistle, signalling for the brakes to be set. There was no chance whatsoever. The cowcatcher snagged the second crosstie (embedding fibres that would be found when the engine was raised). The engine slewed further to the right, pushing and crushing the crossties ahead of it. The right buffer beam crashed into the side lattice, leaving a smear of fresh paint and tearing out the structure that joined the top and bottom chords of the bridge. Bereft of its vertical supports, and with the engine pushing the needle beams of the floor ahead of it like a giant wave, the bridge was already collapsing. As it veered to the right and downward the engine's smokestack left a sooty smudge on the lattice, showing that it had already sunk more than three feet below track level.

As it fell, the engine continued to twist to the right and crashed into the frozen surface of the canal. Carrying a portion of the bridge floor and the tender with it and ending up virtually upside down, partially buried in the mud beneath the ice and water. The baggage car was whipsawed in the opposite direction down the embankment and across the surface of the ice toward the bay.

The first passenger car, in which virtually everybody inside perished, ran into the open gap where the bridge had stood. Momentum carried it outward and gravity carried it downward. When the leading end hit the ice the forward impetus made its bulk rise vertically and then, performing a somersault, smack into the ice roof first with a sickening thud. The second car, now moving a little slower, tipped over the edge and landed solidly on its leading face, to stand wedged more or less vertically against the pier of the bridge. The front end of the car pierced the ice at the relatively shallow edge of the canal, and virtually all the fittings, heavy chairs, upholstery, lamps, and passengers slid the length of the car to jam in a half-submerged mass.

The Inquest

For a few seconds the air was rent with the sounds of screeching metal, breaking timbers, splintering glass, the deep explosions of rapidly escaping steam deep below the canal, and the involuntary screams of sudden panic and instant anguish. Then, as so often is remarked upon is similar circumstances, the cacophony of catastrophe was briefly replaced, while all seemed to hold their breath, by an eerie pall of silence.

EPILOGUE

That momentary silence in the deep, cold twilight of March 12, 1857, is perhaps a fitting epilogue to the story of the disaster. The victims, the railway, and the event seem to have slipped silently into history, making little more impression than a snowflake might make on the still, sullenly flowing waters of the Desjardins Canal.

Conjuring up the full horror of the death of those sixty persons is difficult today. Even if they had been spared to live to a ripe old age, almost all would still have passed away more than a century ago. But somehow it seems like the deaths of so many should have made a deeper impression on our collective history — or at least our folklore.

The bridge itself was quickly reconstructed, and in a manner clearly designed to engender a greater degree of reassurance in the travelling public. The *Hamilton Spectator* of Thursday, March 22, 1860, reported the testing of the new Desjardins Canal Swing Bridge, as follows:

> Yesterday morning, the Chief Engineer of the Great Western Railway, George Lowe Reid, in company

> with Directors Brydges, Becher, Reynolds and Gates, as well as a number of citizens, proceeded by special train to the new bridge for the purpose of testing its stability and trustworthiness. The test, we are happy to say was of the most satisfactory character, leaving no room for doubt that the bridge is as strong as possible and capable of bearing a weight six times heavier than can be put on it at one time.

Two of the heaviest freight engines in the company's service, the Titan and the Pollux, were selected to test the bridge. These engines, with their tenders fully equipped, weighed upwards of one hundred tons each, and though the bearings at the ends of the bridge were only temporarily adjusted, the deflection was only three tenths of an inch. To further assuage still-fresh emotions, the newspaper reported in detail the reassuring specifications of the new structure:

> The bridge consists of two tubular girders of wrought iron, the line of railway passing between them, supported by wrought iron floor beams, which rest on the bottom flanges of the girders. The clear span is 66 feet. The girders are nine feet in height over the turntables 3 foot 6 inches at their extremities, and two feet in widths having double webs of solid plate connecting top and bottom flanges. The weight of the girders and floor beams is 62 1/2 tons, that of the turntable and gearing, 30 tons, and the flooring, 15 tons, making a total of 107 1/2 tons. The flooring is 31 inch oak plank, laid crosswise, in preference to iron which is generally used. This is brought up flush with the rails, so that if a train should happen to de-rail, there would be no drop from rail to floor. The heaviest load that can ever be brought to bear upon the bridge will

Epilogue

only strain the girders to the extent of 3 1/2 tons per square inch, while their breaking point is 20 tons per square inch. The cost of the structure will be almost $20,000. The ironwork was manufactured by Messrs. Fairbairn & Son of Manchester, who sent out with it, one of their most trustworthy foremen, Mr. Lambert, to superintend the erection. The turning apparatus is of the most simple construction and can be worked with the greatest ease by one man. The swing bridge over the Welland Canals immediately below Lock 12 in Merritton, which is nearly finished, is of the same design, but smaller in size.

* * *

In the immediate aftermath, there were plans to erect a suitable memorial. A site was selected and a monument designed that would cost $5,000 (fully one-quarter of the replacement cost of the bridge itself). Interest was high and photographs of the artist's conception were displayed in public places. It was never built.

Burlington Heights is an area of great historic interest. Today you will see a plethora of brass plaques attached to rocks, mounted on tall posts, and affixed to fences. There are memorials to those who died of cholera and to the valiant soldiers of the War of 1812. There is a substantial sign attesting to the military significance of Hamilton Harbour. There are several recognizing the skilled bureaucrats who designed the landscaping. But there is no mention at all of the tragic train accident, although one can stand on the high level bridge and contemplate the very same abutments over which the train passed so many years ago.

At the water level that oversight was remedied a decade or so ago, when a new recreational trail was constructed linking the shores of Burlington Bay with Cootes Paradise, passing directly under the current bridge. Along the path interpretive signs remind strollers of the one-time existence of the extensive facilities of the Great Western Railway, and directly under the bridge a marker provides a capsule description of the disaster, including one of the contemporary photographs. The impassive masonry structure of the abutments is instantly recognizable — unchanged over the past century and a half. It's possible to scramble up and run a hand over those rough stone blocks. There, beside the dank, dark chasm through which the canal still runs, you can picture the scene as it must have been on that horrible night.

For many years there was only one other sign — strangely incongruous in such an isolated setting. It simply warned of the danger of the fast currents running beneath the apparently placid surface, and provided a body count of those who have drowned in recent years. Death never seems very far away from the Desjardins Canal.

If you walk a few hundred feet to the old Hamilton Cemetery, among the graves of a number of the victims you can find the fine memorial to Engineer Burnfield and Fireman Knight, erected at the expense of the Railway Brotherhood, not the Great Western. In keeping with the anonymity that has enveloped the tragedy, the wording has been almost completely obliterated by the weather and vandals stole the fine brass replica of a locomotive that once surmounted the monument many decades ago.

If you travel to St. Davids, near Niagara Falls, you can find the memorial to Samuel Zimmerman. Details of his death are inscribed — almost scratched — into the reverse side of his first wife's tombstone. Zimmerman, whose wealth and power seemed all encompassing in the 1850s, is scarcely accorded the smallest footnote in the history of the time.

Today the catastrophe, like so many of the events in the astounding era that preceded Canada's Confederation, seems of little national importance. Yet the economic imperative behind Confederation was the drive to open up North American commerce. In that, the Great Western Railway played, however briefly, a key role. The seamless

Epilogue

continental integration of technological and engineering know-how was what drove railroad expansion — exemplified by the construction of the GWR in Canada — which persuaded people to consider more strategic political unions. The internationalization of financial markets, allowing companies like the Great Western to place shares in Canadian, U.S. and European markets, was what enabled enterprise to expand beyond merely local boundaries. The railways were also what created ever-expanding markets — hence the presence of the Thorold ploughmaker Morley on the ill-fated train. The already well-developed Canadian administrative structure — epitomized by the rigorous inquiries into the disaster and the railway's record — was what enabled the legislative process that lead to Confederation. Above all, the people of Canada, as well as the soon-to-be amalgamated Maritime provinces, were the progenitors of Confederation, then only a decade in the future. The 4:10 train to Hamilton represented an unfortunate snapshot of the lawyers and politicians, the financiers and the contractors, the rich and the poor, who would have been among the founding participants of Confederation had tragedy not plunged them into eternal silence.

Zimmerman's final resting place. Carved into the reverse of his first wife's stone, are the words: "SAMUEL ZIMMERMAN, Born Huntingdon PA 1815, Contractor and Banker, Benefactor of the Town of Clifton, killed at DES JARDINS CANAL C.W. Mar. 12, 1857."
COURTESY OF RICK BERKETA.

A NOTE ON SOURCES

Given that more than a hundred and fifty years have now elapsed since the tragedy at the Desjardins Canal, the challenge of compiling an accurate record of the precursors of the disaster as well as a complete description of the events themselves might seem daunting. It is and it isn't. There is a surprisingly large volume of immediate reports and official records available. The difficulty is in placing those resources in context.

The problem is not what is written, but what was thought unnecessary to write at the time. What everybody knew and understood. The role and responsibility of a public company was very different then than it is today. The distinction between the individual and public interests of politicians was poles apart from what would be expected today. People "knew" about influential figures, but there were few first-hand interviews and biographies were produced only after an individual's persona had been developed. What people "knew" was generated through third-hand conversations and newspaper commentaries. However, even the newspapers themselves were often political organs, established explicitly to promote a particular philosophy.

When it comes to the disaster itself, the loss of life and the impact on community, the available information is abundant. Even in the 1850s the *Hamilton Spectator* had become a daily newspaper and the contemporary and comprehensive reports of the accident, the aftermath, and the inquest provide a detailed account of the events.

In addition to its regular production, the *Spectator* issued special editions that were rushed to other centres, such as Toronto, but were also issued in the thousands for transport to New York and, via the steamship *Persia*, the United Kingdom and Europe. Based on this material a ten-page pamphlet, titled *The Great Railway Catastrophe*, was authored by Harriet Annie Wilkins and published shortly after the incident. A more comprehensive fifty-two-page booklet, *Full Details of the Railway Disaster of the 12th of March 1857 at the Desjardins Canal*, was published by William A. Shepard & Co and extensively collated the daily reports, augmented by capsule biographies.

Many other newspapers in what is today southwestern Ontario reprinted articles from the *Hamilton Spectator*, augmented by biographical sketches of notable victims who happened to be local residents. The scale of the disaster made it international news and papers like *The New York Times* and *The Times of London* provided coverage that was, not surprisingly, of much more limited substance.

Canadian newspapers were sometimes aligned with various political interests and hence provide coverage with differing sympathies. The *Spectator*, being Hamilton based, was widely viewed as pro–Great Western. The *Toronto Leader* favoured the Grand Trunk and was somewhat less sympathetic. William Lyon McKenzie's *Weekly Message* was openly antagonistic to Great Western interests as well as fervently anti-capitalist.

As noted in the text, Samuel Zimmerman is a somewhat enigmatic figure in Canadian history. When he was alive his international stature was sufficiently recognized that Britain's *Times of London* featured his death in the headline reporting the disaster. He was exceedingly well-known in Canadian business and political circles of the day as a man of great stature and influence, but his standing

A Note on Sources

following his death seems to have quickly dissipated — as evidenced by his humiliating interment in his first wife's crypt without even a simple memorial for many decades.

Contemporary details of his funeral were widely reprinted throughout the region from the account given by the *Hamilton Spectator*, and biographical details were substantially modelled on the account given in *Details of the Railway Disaster of the 12th of March 1857 at The Desjardins Canal*.

Over the past century and a half there have been relatively few efforts to fill Zimmerman's biographical void and those that have been made have attempted to recapture his substantial contribution to what is now Niagara Falls, Ontario. One of the more consequential source is R.W. Geary's "Samuel Zimmerman 1815–1857," published in *Welland County Historical Society Papers and Records, Vol. III*. The Niagara Falls Public Library has established a clipping file of newspaper retrospective articles published over the years. Emma Currie, in *The story of Laura Secord and Canadian Reminiscences*, published in 1900, devotes several pages to Zimmerman.

The chief difficulty with these sources is that they all draw on essentially the same root material that was encapsulated in coverage of his death — the simple facts of his birth and commercial accomplishments. The complex business and political operations that underlay these successes is not discussed. Excellent modern entries in the *Dictionary of Canadian Biography* and its electronic equivalent, although brief, do provide more substantial context.

"The History and Notes of the Zimmerman Bank," authored under the aegis of the National Currency Museum at the Bank of Canada, provide intriguing, albeit somewhat esoteric, insight into Zimmerman's financial manipulations. A taste of the intrigue associated with Zimmerman's last project, the Canada Southern Railway, can be found in legislative records and in published correspondence from Isaac Buchanan held by Library and Archives Canada.

Regional newspapers, while reprinting *Hamilton Spectator* reports augmented them with additional detail on local notables.

For example, the *Kingston British Whig*, March 18, 1957, published added information about Captain Sutherland and on Adam Ferrie. A locally published history of the James Street Baptist Church proved a useful resource on the life and beliefs of Alfred Booker. Entries in the *Canadian Biographical Dictionary* helped illuminate the careers of other casualties — augmented by name-by-name web searches.

Thomas C. Keefer's *Philosophy of Railroads and Other Essays 1848–50* (Reprint, Toronto: University of Toronto Press, 1972) provides a comprehensive analysis of how the establishment of railways in Canada could dramatically impact economic prospects, as well as sounding the murky depths of "railway morality."

Most railway histories of Canada cover the conception, construction, and operations of the Great Western Railway — typically in the context of the Grand Trunk, of which it was an early collaborator, a later competitor, and eventually a subsumed unit. The convoluted politics and behind-the-scenes scheming that were so typical of Canadian railway development are sometimes difficult to unravel from these sources. "The Early Years of the Great Western Railway 1833–1857" by Russell D. Smith, published in *Ontario History* in 1968, provides a very straightforward chronology of the challenges associated with the railway's development.

A sense of some of the rancor and conflict between Canadian and British interests can be deduced from *Great Western Railway of Canada Special Report of the Board of Directors to the English Shareholders* and *Reply of the Directors to the Report of the Committee of Investigation Appointed 30th October, 1873*. Both are available on microfiche at the Toronto Reference Library.

The astonishing early safety record of the Great Western is detailed in Appendix 11 of the Thirteenth Volume of the *Journals of the Legislative Assembly of the Province of Canada Session 1854–55*, available at Library and Archives Canada and some reference libraries.

A considerable literature exists worldwide dealing with railway accidents. Many highlight the melodramatic horrors of such incidents while others attempt to unravel the causes and suggest the means of minimizing future impacts. An early example of the latter is Charles Francis Adams, Jr., *Notes on Railroad Accidents* (New York: G.P. Putnam's Sons, 1879).

While hardly light reading, Squire Whipple's *An Elementary and Practical Treatise on Bridge Building* (New York: D. Van Nostrand, 1847) provides a fascinating contrast with the then-widespread ignorance respecting railway engineering — the more so, given the author's prominent connection with the Desjardins Canal Bridge.

INDEX

Numbers in italics refer to images and their captions.

Accidents
   Angola, New York, 154
   Ashtabula, Ohio, 154, 164, 165
   GWR first fatality, 135
   GWR incident at Baptiste Creek, 143–44, 145–46
   GWR Lobo Collision with livestock, 140–41
   GWR Thorold boy injured, 142
   Long Branch, New Jersey, 155–56
   Norwalk, New, Jersey, 66, 161
   Staplehurst, Kent, 156
   Tay Bridge, Scotland, 159–60

Barrett, Edward, 15, 26
Benedict, Roswell, 60, 63, 64, 127–30
Benson, Thomas, 86–87, 88
Booker, Major Alfred Junior, 28, 78, 136
Booker, Reverend Alfred, 17, 37, 50, 76–77, 204
Brydges, Charles John "C.J.," 37, 49, 86, *101*, 130, 131, 133, 135, 141, 147–48, 149, 168, 173, 195–96
Buchanan, Peter, 101, 107, 108, 130, 203

Burnfield, Alexander, 15, 20, 21, 23, 49–50, 183, 189, 190, 192, 198

Canada Southern Railway, 13, 66, 203
Clarke, T.C., 167, 173
Cobourg and Peterborough Railway, 63–64, 88
Crombie, David, 25–26, 27, 28, 191

Desjardins Canal, 9, 18, 19, 21, 33, 45, 66, 70, 75, 88, 93, 100, 101, 110–11, 117, 123, 124, 135, 136, 144, 160–63, 165, 176, 180, 181, 183, 184, 189
Doyle, Timothy, 34, 71, 88, 90
Duffey, Michael, 27

Ferrie, Adam, 8, 50, 51, 79, *80*, 81, 83, 204
Ferrie, Colin, 112

Garrick, William, 32, 33, 178
Great Western Railway (GWR), 10, 13, *14*, *16*, 20, 21, 26, 28, 32, 36, 37, 56, 65–66, 67, 72, 78, 86, 95, *97*, 108, 120, 121, 123, 131, 136, 137, 146, 147, 162, 171, 195–96, 198, 199, 204

Heise, Reverend Theodore, 49, 90, 91
Henderson, John, 49, 85, 86
House, Diana, 28, 34

Keefer, Thomas, 57, 63–64, 173, 174–75, 186, *187*, 204
Knight, George, 23, 42, 190, 198

Mackenzie, William Lyon, 11, 42, *43*, 102, 103, 118, 168
MacNab, Sir Allan Napier, 18, *43*, 50, 56, 59, 67, 78, 81, 82, *97*, 98, 99, 100, *101*, 102, 103, 104, 107, 108, 109, 110, *111*, 112, 113, 117, 118, 138, 174–75
Marshall, W.R., 29–30, 35
Middlemis, Alexander ("That Noble Fellow"), 36
Milne, R., 37, 169, 170, *170*, 171
Morley, John Thorold, 72, 84, 85, 199
Muir, William, 26, 176–77
Municipal Act of 1849, 112

Niagara Suspension Bridge, 166

Osler, Britton, 44, 45, *46*, 47
Osler, Featherstone, Junior, 45, 47

Osler, Reverend Featherstone, Senior, 44, 45,
Osler, William, 47
Oxford, locomotive, 15, *16*, *19*, 20, 23, 47, 112, 135, 139, 176, 178, 183, 184, 185, 188, 189, 190, *115*, 117, *125*, 126, 129, 150, 151, 162–63, 165, 166, 167, 175, *187*, 189, 198, *199*, 202, 203

Persia, 38, 117, 202

Richardson, Edwin, 28

Schenectady Locomotive Works, *19*, 20
Sevier, Edward, 27
Spaulding, Ira, 64, 129
Street, Thomas C., 15
Sutherland, James, 15, 50, 72, 73, 91, *92*, 93, 94, 204

Twelve Mile Creek trestle, 134, 142
Twohy, Henry, 14, 93–94

Wade, Ralph, 85
Whipple, Squire, 164–65, 166, 167, 177, 180, 181, 182, 183, 186, *188*, 205

Zimmerman, Samuel, 7, 8, 11, 13–15, 31–32, 37, 38, 45, 51, 52, 53, *54*, *55*, 56, 57, 58, 59, 60–61, *62*, 63, *64*, 65, 66–73, *74*, 88, 93, 98,

Of Related Interest

Losing the Empress
A Personal Journey
David Creighton
978-1-550023404 | $24.99

The *Empress of Ireland*'s last voyage ended on May 29, 1914, when she was rammed by a Norwegian coal-carrier in a fog patch on the St. Lawrence River near Rimouski. For David Creighton, her voyage still continues.

In *Losing the Empress*, Creighton delves into the lives of his grandparents — Salvation Army officers who were lost on the *Empress* — and the lives of their five orphaned children who would soon be plunged into the First World War. His discoveries reveal amazing details about the *Empress*, which sank in fourteen minutes with a greater loss of life than the *Titanic* disaster.

Shipwreck nostalgia, last voyage dinners, Salvationists, the British Empire, and the world wars fought to preserve it; everything comes into focus when the author joins *Titanic* discoverer Robert Ballard on a film shoot at the sunken liner's site. *Losing the Empress* lyrically traces a personal journey into the past and into the future.

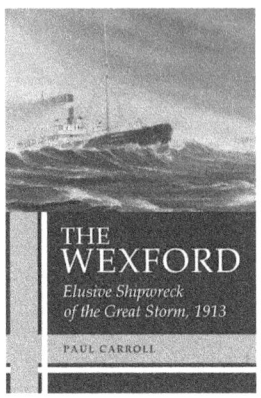

The Wexford
Elusive Shipwreck of the Great Storm, 1913
Paul Carroll
978-1-554887361 | $30.00

The steamer *Wexford*, with her flared bow, tall masts, and her open, canvas-sided hurricane deck, charmed spectators as she carried cargo across the Great Lakes. The romance and adventure of her British and French history in the South American trade followed her. Under newly appointed twenty-four-year-old captain, Bruce Cameron, her fateful final voyage was punctuated with opportunities to be saved from destruction, but his persistence in trying to make port at Goderich led to tragedy — a victim of the storm of 1913. Over a period of eighty-seven years she eluded many efforts to locate her remains, but was finally discovered in 2000 by a sailor using a fish-finding device. Since then she has been visited by thousands, but sadly plundered. Our story traces her history from her British origins in 1883, through the transition to become a "Laker," the eventful storm, the search, her ultimate discovery in southern Lake Huron, and the controversy over how she should be protected.

Available at your favourite bookseller.

Visit us at
Dundurn.com
Definingcanada.ca
@dundurnpress
Facebook.com/dundurnpress

www.ingramcontent.com/pod-product-compliance
Lightning Source LLC
Chambersburg PA
CBHW031312150426
43191CB00005B/201